NON-TRADITIONAL
AGRICULTURE AND
ECONOMIC DEVELOPMENT

NON-TRADITIONAL AGRICULTURE AND ECONOMIC DEVELOPMENT

The Brazilian Soybean Expansion, 1964–1982

Anthony B. Soskin

PRAEGER

New York
Westport, Connecticut
London

Library of Congress Cataloging-in-Publication Data

Soskin, Anthony B.
  Non-traditional agriculture and economic development : the
Brazilian soybean expansion, 1964-1982 / Anthony B. Soskin.
    p. cm.
  Bibliography: p. **14783 21 JAN 2002**
  Includes index.
  ISBN 0-275-92803-9 (alk. paper)
  1. Soybean industry – Brazil – History – 20th century.
2. Agriculture and state – Brazil – History – 20th century.
3. Exports – Brazil – History – 20th century. 4. Brazil – Economic
policy. 5. Brazil – Economic conditions – 1964-1985. I. Title.
HD9235.S62B784   1988
338.1'7334'0981 – dc19   87-30872

Library of Congress Catalog Card Number: 87-30872
ISBN: 0-275-92803-9

First published in 1988

Praeger Publishers, One Madison Avenue, New York, NY 10010
A division of Greenwood Press, Inc.

Printed in the United States of America

The paper used in this book complies with the
Permanent Paper Standard issued by the National
Information Standards Organization (Z39.48-1984).

10 9 8 7 6 5 4 3 2 1

To Penny

Contents

Tables and Figures

FIGURES

Preface

This study seeks to examine the issues involved in the promotion of a non-traditional agricultural crop as a means of furthering economic development. It traces the history and impact of the expansion of the Soybean crop on the Brazilian economy between 1964 and 1982. In particular the study seeks to identify the implications for Brazilian economic development of the support for the rapid growth of a non-traditional agricultural crop such as soybeans, and to link the Brazilian experience to some of the classical theories of economic development.

The work analyzes the objectives of the Brazilian government over the period, the agricultural policies and the policy instruments put into place to achieve these objectives, as well as the micro and macro impact upon the relevant sectors of the economy. In addition the study examines the importance of the soybean expansion upon Brazil's foreign trade.

The conclusions drawn by the analysis demonstrate that the considerable success in achieving such a rapid and significant expansion of the soybean crop was not without drawbacks. The soybean crop is shown to have made a positive contribution to Brazil's foreign trade and the balance of payments. However, the linkages formed by the soybean economy are substantially with the modern sector rather than the traditional. The expansion was based largely upon imported technology, and much of the growth was shown to have been at the expense of traditional domestic staple crops upon which the poorer groups in Brazilian society depend.

Although the soybean crop made a significant contribution to agricultural growth and the increase in overall farm incomes, the divisions within agriculture and between regions were in fact deepened. Little was achieved in terms of redressing the inequities in farm structure nor did the expansion of the soybean crop act to stem the flow of the rural poor moving to the urban centers.

Map of Brazil

CEARÁ — State
AMAPÁ — Territory

NON-TRADITIONAL
AGRICULTURE AND
ECONOMIC DEVELOPMENT

1
Research Area
and Objectives of Study

INTRODUCTION

Brazil is one of the world's largest countries in terms of land area. It is the free world's seventh largest economy as measured by Gross National Product (GNP), or ninth largest including the non-market economies of the Soviet Union and China (World Bank, 1985). Nevertheless, in terms of GNP per capita, Brazil falls only midway among the middle income countries; its highly sophisticated modern industrial sector with its remarkable record of high economic growth masks enduring underdevelopment in a very significant rural sector.

Although Brazil is now a highly industrialized economy and agriculture ceased to be Brazil's leading sector in the 1940s, 30 percent of the working population remain in agriculture (Table 1-1). Within Brazil disparities abound: there is a modern prosperous agriculture in specific areas yet traditional subsistence agriculture in others; wealthy and powerful landowners in the modern sector yet a substantial proportion of rural poor, to which one must add the growing numbers of urban poor, and a highly skewed land tenure system leaving vast tracts of potentially productive lands in the hands of traditional landowners with little incentive for technological improvement while subsistence farming is maintained in often inhospitable and decaying conditions. With all this, agricultural and food policy takes on a mantle of high importance.

Since virtually the beginning of Brazil's history, exports have played a vital role in her growth and development, and no less so today. Agricultural products make up some 47 percent of Brazilian exports. Of these soybeans and soybean products account for 10.8 percent of the total and 23.2 percent of agricultural exports. Brazil is a country of immense contrasts, geographic, demographic and economic. Its land area amounts to 8.5 million square kilometers, making it the third largest nation in the world in terms of geographic area. Some 2.4 million square kilometers are used for agriculture in some form, 1.63 million in permanent pasture and 75 million hectares of crop land. Of this, in turn, 8.2 million hectares are planted in soybeans.

Table 1-1   Brazil: Economically Active Population (%)

Sector	1950	1960	1970	1980
Agriculture	59.7	52.1	45.1	30.4
Mining	0.7	0.7	0.6	0.6
Manufacturing	12.9	13.7	14.8	17.9
Construction	3.5	3.7	5.9	7.6
Electricity	0.7	0.7	1.0	1.0
Commerce	6.4	8.0	9.3	*
Transport	4.1	5.1	4.3	4.6
Services	12.0	16.0	18.5	*
Wholesale/Retail/Hotels				12.0
Finance/Insurance/Business Services				2.4
Community/Social/Personal Services				23.6

* Service and Commerce sectors re-defined 1980
Source: Latin American Statistical Yearbook—various
        issues, United Nations, New York.

The soybean crop developed in Brazil from virtually nothing, growing from 171,000 hectares in 1960 to the 8.2 million hectares grown in 1982. Whereas 92 percent of the crop was to be found in the state of Rio Grande do Sul in the early 1960s, by the early 1980s it had spread much further afield, both through expansion within the traditional farming areas and as a pioneer crop on the frontier. However, even with this enormous expansion, direct benefits accrued only to farmers in a relatively small sector of the country, for in 1981 71.5 percent of plantings were confined to only two states, Rio Grande do Sul and Parana, with the neighboring states of Sao Paulo and Santa Caterina providing a further 12 percent. With 10.5 percent being grown on the frontier states of Mato Grosso and Mato Grosso do Sul, 94 percent of all plantings were confined, largely for climatic reasons, to a very restricted part of Brazil's agricultural area.

With much of Brazil's rural poor being confined to the northeastern states and the majority of the remaining poor living alongside or within the urban areas, both cropping policy as a whole, and more specifically distribution of crops, were likely to have exerted a profound effect on development within Brazil in its widest sense.

Soybeans, as they are grown in Brazil, are a modern crop, utilizing highly developed husbandry methods and requiring high inputs of a physical and a technical nature, both of which are in short supply in Brazil. The utilization of resources and the transfer of resources between sectors, both within agriculture and outside, are of paramount importance to a developing nation, and Brazil is no exception.

STRUCTURE AND OBJECTIVES OF THIS STUDY

Structure

This study concerns the expansion of a non-traditional agricultural crop, soybeans, and the impact it has had on Brazilian agriculture and the economic development of the country. It will examine the growth of the soybean industry in Brazil from its earliest days until the early 1980s, by which time it had reached a point of immense importance in the Brazilian economy. Several authors have examined the last two decades of Brazilian economic development, and there have been numerous benchmark studies of the growth of Brazilian agriculture. In addition, there have been several specific studies of the soybean industry in Brazil (Schultz and Mason, 1976; Duran, 1979; Gulliver, 1981; Williams and Thompson, 1984a). The purpose of this volume is to examine the history of the expansion of the Brazilian soybean crop in the context of some of the fundamental theories of agricultural development, to pull together the threads of some of the earlier research work, to investigate how and why this expansion occurred, and to study some of the implications for Brazilian agriculture and the development process.

This study will start with an outline of Brazil's general geographic and physical makeup, factors of paramount importance in the development potential of Brazilian agriculture. There then follows a brief overview of the general development of the Brazilian economy in order that the importance of the soybean crop may be put in its proper perspective, together with an outline of the role of agriculture in Brazil. Then follows an examination of some of the relevant literature on the role of agriculture in economic development and its application to the case of Brazil. The work will examine the policies of the Brazilian government, including both their impact upon and their implications for the expansion of soybeans. Further sections will trace the growth of the crop in Brazilian agriculture and the micro implications associated with it, including the establishment and rapid growth of Brazil's soybean processing industry. Next some of the macro issues involved will be examined, including the importance to Brazil's foreign trade. The concluding chapters will look at some of the results of the policy interventions, examine alternative scenarios, and attempt to draw conclusions regarding the circumstances surrounding the soybean expansion and the implications for the development of Brazil.

Objectives

The primary objective of this volume is to trace the expansion of the soybean crop in Brazil and identify its impact on Brazilian agriculture and the Brazilian economy. Specifically the work intends to:

1. Identify the policy background that provided the environment for such a rapid expansion of a single crop.
2. Identify the resources diverted to soybean production and the effect this had on the growing of other crops.
4. Non-Traditional Agriculture
3. Examine the contribution the soybean crop has made to Brazilian exports and her balance of trade.
4. Examine the distributive effects of the expansion of soybeans within the economy.
5. Assess the options which were open to the Brazilian government and the alternative results which might have occurred.
6. Assess the success, in terms of the development of Brazil, of the concentration on and the rapid expansion of the soybean crop.

THE GEOGRAPHY OF BRAZIL

Before looking at the economic development of Brazil it is imperative to have a clear understanding of its geography and physical characteristics. Brazil's very development was heavily influenced by these, as was its past and present pattern of agriculture. Brazil is one of the world's largest countries in terms of land area, exceeded only by the Soviet Union, Canada, China, and the United States. It is the larger part of South America, occupying some 43.2 percent of the continent (see Table 1-2).

Table 1-2   South America: Land Area, Population, and GNP

Country	Land Area (000 Ha)	%	Population Total (mill)	Growth Rate 1960-70	Growth Rate 1970-80	Per Capita ($)	GNP Growth Rate 1960-80
Brazil	851,200	47.8	118.7	2.9	2.2	2,050	5.1
Argentina	276,689	15.5	27.7	1.4	1.6	2,390	2.2
Colombia	113,891	6.4	26.7	3.0	2.3	1,180	3.0
Peru	128,522	7.2	17.4	2.8	2.6	930	1.1
Venezuala	91,205	5.1	14.9	3.4	3.3	3,630	2.6
Chile	75,695	4.3	11.1	2.1	1.7	2,150	1.6
Ecuador	28,356	1.6	8.0	3.0	3.0	1,270	4.5
Bolivia	109,858	6.2	5.8	2.3	2.5	570	2.1
Uruguay	17,751	1.0	2.9	1.0	0.3	2,810	1.4
Paraguay	40,695	2.3	2.7	2.5	3.2	1,300	3.2
Guyana	21,497	1.2	0.8	1.8	1.5	570 [1]	1.9 [2]
Surinam	16,327	0.9	0.5	2.6	2.4	1,360 [1]	-0.6 [2]
French Guyana	9,100	0.5	0.1	2.9	2.7	1,820 [1]	0.0 [2]
SOUTH AMERICA	1,780,786	100.0	237.3				
USA	936,300		222.7	1.3	1.0	11,360	2.3
Canada	997,600		23.9	1.8	1.1	10,130	3.3
United Kingdom	24,500		55.9	0.1	0.1	7,920	2.2

[1] 1976 [2] 1960-1976
Source: World Development Report--various issues, World Bank, Washington, D.C.

Settled by Europeans as far back as the fifteenth century, Brazil had long been regarded as a land of plenty, blessed with an abundance of fertile land and natural resources, yet in many aspects it failed to live up to the promises of early explorers. Many parts remain, even today, fairly sparsely settled, with the majority of Brazilians still living within 400 miles of the coast. Even within this coastal belt, where some of the earliest settlements were situated, the land tenure structure has caused the land to remain extensively farmed with substantial potential for further intensification.

There has long been a gradual movement toward the interior, and this has accelerated in recent years; the frontier, which has over the centuries provided Brazil with an outlet for its territorial ambitions, has been substantially eroded. The construction of the highway system, the building of the nation's new capital, Brasilia, the agricultural development in the Center-West, and the movement of population along the banks of the Amazon have all done their part to bring the whole country closer to full development. However, in spite of this there remain areas of Brazil which still display the characteristics found in some of the world's least developed nations.

The reasons for the enormous differences within the country are many and complex. Some constitue a carryover from the original social and political infrastructure installed by the Portuguese colonists when the country was first settled; also a factor is the diversity and settlement pattern of the people who populated the nation in its early years. Other reasons stem from the uneven economic development of the country which caused a series of economic booms, the advantages from which were all too soon lost in the economic retrogressions which followed.

The Brazilian settlement pattern exhibits many anomalies in terms of resource endowment. Areas of dense agricultural settlement in the northeast on poorer lands are subject to flood and drought, while well-watered lands further south stand almost empty. Eroded and impoverished lands are intensively cultivated whereas fertile and accessible areas, such as along the Amazon river and its tributaries, are still barely used. Nevertheless people found the means to move substantial distances within the coastal area to form the modern cities of Rio de Janeiro and Sao Paulo, often leaving in their wake the once promising centers of the early settlement (Henshall and Momsen, 1974).

Much of the problem can be found within the physical characteristics of Brazil, including a lack of natural transportation routes to the interior, absence of physical possibilities for leaving the coastal strip, and lack of lands that settle and cultivate easily. All these factors, so deficient in Brazil, were prevalent in the United States during its similar period of development. Brazil has no extreme climatic conditions, but the very substantial degree of difference in climate and soil quality that does exist, and particularly the enormous distances and difficulties in reaching back to the markets, may have dampened the enthus- iasm with which the early explorers regarded the "land of plenty" in an agricultural sense.

Although similar in territorial extent to the United States, Brazil differs considerably both in climate and in physical topography. The majority of its territory consists of geologically ancient uplands. Much of the land, about 57 percent, is on a plateau varying between 650 and 3000 feet above sea level. About 40 percent occurs as lowlands below the 650 feet contour, and the remainder is all above 3000 but less than 10,000 feet. In the north of the country the land rises from east to west; but parallel with the coast line, in the center and south, the land drops off sharply toward the Atlantic. This slope, known as the Great Escarpment, kept access to the interior difficult and is often held to be a fundamental reason for the relatively slow movement of the population inland on the south-central plateau prior to this century. Beyond the escarpment is a plateau which slopes gradually towards the west (Henshall and Momsen, 1974).

Unlike the United States, Brazil is not blessed with the comprehensive river system which contributed so much to the development of the North American interior. Apart from the Amazon, which runs from the Peruvian Andes, through the Brazilian jungle to the fertile Amazon delta in the northeast corner of Brazil, most of the principal rivers are found in the central or southern parts of the country, rising near the coast and flowing inward, eventually draining into the Argen- tinean river system. The Sao Francisco river does rise in the south, but flows north, parallel to the coast for more than one thousand miles before turning east and discharging into the sea. Many of Brazil's rivers pass through the Great Escarpment, dropping rapidly and making navigation impract- ical for large vessels. In Brazil, only the Amazon is navig- able throughout its length; however, it unites only the least exploited region of the country.

Brazil's most accessible and historically productive lowlands, which are found on the banks of the Amazon and along the northeastern Atlantic coast, are non-contiguous and dominated by hot, humid climates. In the Amazon area, soils consist of seasonally inundated plains interdispersed with less fertile soils. The estuary zone itself is reduced in usefulness because of seasonal or tidal flooding. Although the coastal mountains, north of Salvador, are neither high nor steep, they have the effect of triggering precipitation from the trade winds in an otherwise moisture deficient area. Further south, the mountains become much higher and more rugged, causing excessive precipitation along the coast and intermittent droughts in the interior (Henshall and Momsen, 1974).

In the southernmost portion of Brazil, the escarpment bends westward producing a line of low hills along the northern part of Rio Grande do Sul where there are some of the few substantial areas of family-run mixed farms in southern Brazil. Here the land was colonized by immigrants from Germany and Italy during the wave of immigration that took place during the last two decades of the nineteenth century. The coastal plain then merges with the northern-most extension of the Uruguay and Argentinean "pampas" producing large, traditional areas of grazing which in recent years have given way substantially to the introduction of arable crops, especially soybeans (Soskin, 1981). Although the grasslands in southern Rio Grande do Sul are also known as pampas, they are in fact subtropical rather than temperate and the soils are therefore less fertile and the climate less hospitable to temperate crops, as was discovered through Brazil's efforts to become a significant grower of wheat. The remaining lowlands in Brazil are found along the Paraguay river and consist of a seasonally inundated alluvial plain.

Where the Brazilian plateau extends into the subtropics and frost occurs, the natural vegetation consists of pine forests and meadowland, with the productivity of the area depending on the underlying strata and the steepness of the slopes. Its most fertile parts occur in the southern and western parts of the region, extending discontinuously to the forests of northern Parana and western Sao Paulo. From there they continue to the "Triangle" of western-most Minas Gerais and into southern Goias. The full value of these potentially fertile volcanic soils is not uniformly realizable because of dryness in the north, frosts to the south, and higher temperatures to the west where the plateau declines in elevation (Henshall and Momsen, 1974).

The bulk of the Brazilian highlands centers on Goias and Mato Gross do Sul where they are known as the Central Plateau; the soils here are capable of producing good crops and this area formed the frontier during the 1970s when rapid development of cultivation took place on former grazing land This area was responsible for much of the later expansion of the soybean crop area. Further north, however, moisture becomes a problem and the soils are inherently less fertile. Consequently, Brazil's climate, soil types, topography and access to its heartland present many difficulties and are much to blame for the slow and uneven pace of agricultural development, so very different from its North American counterpart, the midwestern states.

BRAZILIAN ECONOMIC DEVELOPMENT AND THE ROLE OF AGRICULTURE

To provide a base for our understanding of the story of
the growth of Brazil's soybean economy, the development of
Brazilian agricultural policies, and the patterns of agricultural progress Brazil has made over the last two decades,
it is necessary, to have not only some conception of the
physical characteristics of the country, but also an understanding of the history of the economic development of Brazil
and the role of agriculture therein. There are interesting
parallels with the concentration upon other single export
crops at several stages in the four centuries since the
founding of the Brazilian nation.

As mentioned above, Brazil has long been regarded as a
land of plenty; not only did this reputation arise from its
immense land area and its apparent wealth of natural resources but it emanated from series of waves of enormous
growth, based on a single agricultural or extractive product.
These waves ebbed and flowed like the tide, building up to
magnificent peaks only to disappear to nothing as markets
changed and Brazil failed to capitalize, perhaps through lack
of will or perhaps through lack of ability to consolidate its
advantages. Brazil was primarily an export-oriented, agricultural or extractive economy, from its earliest settlement
until early in the twentieth century, when the first signs of
the urban industrial complex began to appear. Never having
had a cultural base similar to that of the United States nor
a planned settlement pattern such as developed in the U.S.
heartland, Brazil was primarily an economy designed to benefit its colonial masters and the wealthy landowners who held
the reins of production. This set the pattern until Brazil
became independent and market conditions began to change with
the onset of the first World War. Subsequently industry
began to expand until, in the 1950s, it took over as the
leading sector and became the motor of a growth which has
continued to this day.

Brazil was first settled at the beginning of the sixteenth century by Portuguese and other European pioneers.
The name "Brazil" was derived from Brazil-wood, an important
constituent in the manufacture of dyestuffs in Europe but not
sufficient to encourage settlement or provide any form of
agricultural infrastructure (Baer, 1983). Sugar was the
first major product to be exported from Brazil, commencing in
1530 and lasting until the Brazilian crop no longer could

compete with the shorter distances to market and the more efficient production from the Caribbean (Nicholls, 1969).

Sugar was also the first major crop to provide the impetus for the first wave of settlement and growth commencing in the 1530s. According to Furtado, it was a set of favorable circumstances to which this development was due (Furtado, 1971). The demand for sugar in Europe was rising, and there was already a substantial fund of knowledge among the Portuguese, which derived from their experiences with cane sugar growing and milling equipment on their Atlantic islands. Without this, Furtado writes, the Brazilian experience would have been far harder to attain and much longer in coming. In addition, there was a substantial contribution from the low countries, mainly Dutch, to the expansion of the sugar market in the latter half of the sixteenth century. The Dutch were able to finance a large part of the expansion of Brazil's productive capacity and Portugal was able to provide slave labor from the African slave market. This enabled the early settlers to cope with the severe manpower shortage in the colony. The hot, humid conditions of the northeastern seaboard were ideal for the establishment of sugar plantations, and this led to a rapid spread of cultivation over the whole coastal area. As the market strengthened, the sugar crop expanded, not by improvements in the production process, but through added inputs in the form of land (expanding on to virgin soils) and labor (by substantially increasing the slave population). Sugar production was mostly based on plantation-style agriculture on very large estates. This was, according to Furtado, the first success story in the agricultural development of Brazil (Furtado, 1971).

The political and economic environment during the early part of the sixteenth century favored the rapid rise and fast growth of agricultural enterprise in Brazil, which laid the foundations of the first substantial settlement. However, the situation changed, first when Portugal was taken over by Spain, and subsequently during the wars between Spain and Portugal in 1580 and 1640, both of which had profound repercussions for Portuguese Latin America. For a quarter of a century (1630-1654) the Dutch occupied the Brazilian northeast, the sugar producing area, and during the period of occupation acquainted themselves with a detailed knowledge of the sugar industry. This in turn led to the Dutch installing and developing a large-scale, competitive sugar industry in the Caribbean. The Caribbean Islands had an immense competitive advantage in terms of closeness to the market centers in Europe. This had serious implications for the Portuguese, breaking their monopoly and causing a dramatic fall in sugar prices. The period of maximum profitability passed, and during the latter half of the seventeenth century exports barely reached 50 percent of the high point in 1650. By 1700, both Portugal and Brazil were finding themselves in a substantial economic decline. This phenomenon of rapid growth and equally rapid decline was to repeat itself several times in the Brazilian experience (Furtado, 1971).

During the previous hundred years of rapid expansion up to 1650, the Brazilian sugar industry had given the first impetus to the settlement of the interior. Virtually all the land on the coastal belt had come under the influence of the monoculture of the sugar crop, but the colonial settlers and their slaves needed food, fuel, and draught animals. Cattle rearing on land suitable for sugar production was soon prohibited by the crown and hence the economic pressure grew to develop the interior. The incentive was reduced with the contraction of the sugar industry, but by then there was a political need to improve overland communications, particularly in the face of threats from other European powers. Therefore the slow spread of settlement into the interior began, dictated by different pressures at different times, a pattern to be repeated over the next three centuries and continuing to contemporary times (Nicholls, 1969).

The Portuguese regained their independence from Spain in 1640, and the government strove to reach agreement with the Dutch, the then enemy of Spain on the high seas. This resulted in failure, and Portugal turned instead to the British. Henceforward Portugal became more and more reliant on British protection, and in return gave British merchants a considerable degree of preference for their manufactures in Portuguese markets. As Furtado writes, "Portugal became virtually England's commercial vassal, broadly viewed the Portuguese–Brazilian economy of the 18th Century resembled an affiliation with the most rapidly growing economic system of the time, the British" (Furtado, 1971, 35–38).

By the beginning of the eighteenth century, both Portugal and Brazil were suffering economically. Their salvation came with the discovery of gold in Minas Gerais. The gold rush which followed attracted poor colonial settlers and the first of the Portuguese immigrants with limited means. In addition, the excess slave population was moved from the northeast sugar areas down to the goldfields. The gold rush naturally created a burgeoning demand for supplies in the form of food, cattle, and beasts of burden, a demand which by far exceeded anything that existed during the most prosperous years of the sugar industry. This demand revitalized the fledgling cattle areas of the south, and food crops began to appear around the goldfield area in Minas Gerais. The gold boom was spent by the end of the century but its course had inflicted a substantial toll on the agriculture of the northeast. The sugar industry in the Northeast was weak and had suffered from the increasing competition for supplies from the goldfields. Furthermore, the political power base was moved from the northeast to the south when the Brazilian capital moved from Salvador to Rio de Janeiro in 1763. Meanwhile much of the benefit of the gold boom flowed via Portugal to England, where the gainers were the British manufacturers and the British economy.

The Northeast was not entirely neglected, however, with chartered trading companies being set up to promote cotton, tobacco and the rehabilitation of the sugar industry (Nicholls, 1969). There followed a series of events which were to boost the northeastern economy. These included in particular the American War of Independence and the War of 1812 which disrupted England's normal supply sources of cotton and tobacco, the French Revolution and the slave revolt which destroyed the Haitian sugar industry (Nicholls, 1969). Another event of importance was the Napoleonic Wars which brought the Portuguese royal family to Brazil in 1808. As a result, in the period beginning prior to independence in 1822 and continuing to the end of the monarchy, the south withdrew into a subsistence economy with the passing of the gold boom but the Northeast once more underwent considerable growth with the colonies' agricultural exports almost doubling (Furtardo, 1971). However, the new-found prosperity of the northeast was somewhat precarious in nature, relying upon the fluctuating nature of the market for tropical products.

By mid-century (1850) coffee made its appearance on the Brazilian agricultural scene, beginning a completely new age of economic growth which was to last for more than 50 years. The greatest problem facing Brazil at this time was a supply of labor which had come to a dead end (Furtado, 1971, 120). The supply of slaves from Africa had been stopped and there was no alternative in sight. The only way out for development in the late nineteenth century was through international trade. Little credit could be raised by a government of a country whose economy was decaying and whose tax collecting capabilities were therefore restricted (Prado, 1967). By now the sugar market was once more weak, with Cuba, as the main supplier of the North American market, selling three times the quantity of Brazil.

Cotton had become a crop of considerable importance, taking second place in the Brazilian export list. Vast expansion of the textile industry in England during the latter half of the eighteenth century, following the invention of the mechanical loom, saw England's cotton consumption rise from 4.6 million to 26 million pounds. The inability of traditional suppliers to meet this demand set in motion enormous expansion in the Americas, of which Brazil had a not inconsiderable share. However, before long the market for cotton deteriorated sharply. Large-scale production in the United States resulted in prices falling by more than two thirds and left Brazil unable to compete (Prado, 1967).

Therefore, the only really encouraging development in the years between 1822 and 1850 was the first evidence of the potential of coffee. First planted in the Amazon region in 1727, it had spread as far south as Rio de Janeiro but had only been grown on a small scale for domestic consumption. In the years 1821-1830, both sugar and cotton exports still outpaced those of coffee; however, by 1841-1850 the positions had been reversed, with coffee representing 41 percent of total Brazilian exports. Coffee exports continued to grow, but the benefits were heavily biased toward the states of Rio de Janeiro and Sao Paulo; the northeast largely missed the boom. The coffee plant does not thrive on coastal lowlands, but does best on the higher land of the slopes facing the lowland fringe. This was the first significant movement of cultivated crops toward the interior.

However, technical progress in Brazilian agriculture was almost non-existent, with any growth being in quantitative rather than qualitative output. Wasteful and primitive methods of production during the early years were beginning to show up in impoverishment of the soil. No alternatives were on hand other than to abandon cultivations for a period until there was some measure of recovery, but the intervals between crops became longer and longer until eventual exhaustion set in (Prado, 1967).

The low productivity of Brazilian agriculture, the lack of technical improvement and the wholesale loss of substantial expanses of land by large-scale exploitation are emphasized by Prado, who goes onto say that to have changed the system even then would have called for far-reaching economic and perhaps even social reforms. By this time in Brazilian agriculture there were already two discernable sectors, differing completely in character. First, there was large-scale commercial agriculture producing important crops for the export market, and second, there were subsistence farmers supplying the domestic market. It was this pattern of organization of agricultural production that dictated the whole social, economic, and political structure of the country. Similarly, it was this set of socioeconomic factors which formed the basis of the "latifundio" ("fazendas" and plantations) and "minifundios" (subsistence plots) as well as the divisions between export and domestic agriculture that have remained a significant influence on Brazilian agriculture to this day.

The growth of coffee continued unabated, and it was soon to become (and remain for a considerable period) Brazil's principal export crop. Its share of Brazilian exports rose from 19 percent in 1821-1830 to 63 percent by 1881 (Baer, 1983). However the fortuitous growth of such an important single export crop did not lead to the development of the Brazilian economy which one might have expected. Unlike their North American counterparts, the Brazilian landowners who derived huge wealth from their plantations preferred to preserve their European cultural heritage on the South American continent, showing little inclination to develop a separate identity for Brazil but looking continuously back towards Europe for their cultural model. Preferring European goods, they showed little inclination to reinvest their capital either in agriculture or industrialization (Nicholls, 1969).

Manufacturing was prohibited during colonial times, and until 1844 the privileged treaty position granted to England effectively prevented any protection for fledgling industries. Nicholls argues that any efforts to encourage the diversification of the Brazilian economy or develop an infrastructure met with only modest success, having very little support from the agrarian-based power structure (Nicholls, 1969). Baer maintains, however, that in the early years of the new republic there was a considerable school of thought which favored industrialization, claiming that Brazil had to complement its political independence by acquiring some degree of economic independence, and that this could only be achieved by encouraging new industries to produce goods which could replace a large part of Brazil's imports. Pressure led to a measure of tariff protection and behind this protective barrier many small firms were established, but their total output represented only a very small part of Brazil's economic activity (Baer, 1983).

Two additional crops then appeared on the scene and expanded very rapidly. Cacao had been introduced in the middle of the nineteenth century, but not until 1907, when new, high yielding varieties were introduced from Ceylon, did Brazil become competitive in the world market. For a brief time cacao became an important export crop and Brazil a major supplier. The other crop was a native of the Brazilian Amazon region, the rubber plant. With the development of the infant automobile industry at the turn of the century, the world demand for rubber mushroomed. Brazil being the only source lead to a boom of immense proportions in the Amazon jungle regions, creating vast profits for Brazilian and foreign entrepreneurs. Unfortunately for Brazil, by the late 1800s the first commercial plantations had been established in British Colonial Malaya; by 1899 the first supplies from this new source began to appear on the world market. By the 1920s the market was saturated and prices collapsed. Brazil had neither the will nor the ability to compete. Having relied solely on forest rubber trees, and having put no effort into developing the technology required for commercial plantations, Brazil lost its entire share of the world market within a few years.

Nevertheless, the growing population and the success of agriculture in the state of Sao Paulo were beginning to make themselves felt; the state became the hub of Brazilian development, both agricultural and industrial, over the next half century. Huge surpluses from the coffee trade were to dominate Brazilian economic growth until the onset of the second World War. It was this development, and in particular the emergence of the first industrial-urban complex, which provided the impetus for modernization of a still largely static agriculture in the country at large. It was the virgin lands to the west and the improvements in transportation, in particular the opening of Brazil's first rail links, which smoothed the path for the westward development of coffee across the state of Sao Paulo. During the period 1931-1940, Brazil still produced 64 percent of the world's coffee and the state of Sao Paulo contributed 68 percent of this (Nicholls, 1969).

Industrialization began to be encouraged due to a series of external shocks, including several wars, the Great Depression, and periodic foreign exchange problems. Other contributing factors during this period included the lack of employment on the fazendas, releasing labor for the new factories, and also the continuing number of immigrants, some of whom—if they were not on assisted passages—remained in urban areas. The expansion of the railway system and the development of electrical generating capacity, together with the inflow of foreign capital, kept industrialization growing (Baer, 1983).

The outbreak of World War I provided new opportunities for Brazil, as supplies from overseas were interrupted and

foreign competition eliminated.   In the 1920s, according to
Baer, many of the industries created during the war suffered
from high pricing and poor quality.   The world wide Great
Depression had a severe effect on Brazilian exports, but the
pattern of industrial development was set.   The government's
main concern was still the coffee sector.   In the 1930s heavy
over-production of coffee throughout the world led to a
dramatic fall in profitability as markets collapsed.   Brazil
acted to stimulate diversification in both agriculture and
the economy at large while maintaining the coffee support
policy, under which the government had destroyed around   30
percent of total production.   This was eventually to lead to
the loss of a substantial share of the world market (Baer,
1983).
     More significant was the huge injection of purchasing
power, via the support policies, into the coffee economy.   As
Nicholls points out, this came at a time when Brazil was
undergoing a foreign exchange crisis and led to a dramatic
stimulation of the demand for domestic manufactures. During
the 1930s idle capacity was brought into production to satisfy these demands.   World War II was to provide even more
encouragement to manufacturers as it caused another inter-
ruption in supplies from abroad (Nicholls, 1969).
     After the war, in the early 1950s, the first theories
and encouragement for Latin American countries to move toward
wholesale import substitution industrialization (ISI)
appeared on the scene.   Brazil followed this line relig-
iously, bringing in a set of policies to promote domestic
manufacturing. Paramount among these was a complex system of
multiple exchange rates which heavily discriminated, for the
first time, against Brazil's traditional agricultural exports
while favoring the import of certain factors of production.
The purpose of this, it is generally accepted, was to allow
Brazil to divert a large part of foreign exchange earnings
from traditional export crops to general development, in
particular the maintenance of low market prices.   This was a
costly excercise for the agricultural sector; the only crop
to benefit directly from this new policy initiative was
wheat. Eventually the neglect of agriculture resulted in
serious food shortages, with consequent higher prices eventually culminating in a supply crisis in the early 1960s.

2
Review of Literature

INTRODUCTION

There is a substantial fund of literature on the contribution
of agriculture to economic development. Development theories
seek to find a rationale for the past and, as a consequence,
a guide to the future in explaining the course of economic
development.   Some have partial application to Brazil's
historical agricultural development, and others to the contemporary situation.   Presented below is a review of some of
the classical writings on the importance of agriculture in
the development process relevant to the Brazilian situation,
including a theoretical justification for dependence on a
single export crop as a development tool. This will be
followed by an overview of some of the studies of Brazilian
agricultural policy initiatives and their effectiveness.
Finally, an outline describes some of the work done on the
impact of recent, policy-oriented agricultural growth in
Brazil in terms of its general benefit to the country's
economic development.

DEVELOPMENT THEORY: INDUSTRIAL EXPANSION AND AGRICULTURAL MODERNIZATION

Many attempts have been made to find an all-embracing
theory to cover the transition between underdevelopment and a
modern industrialized economy.   According to John Mellor,
early economic development involves a major transformation of
an economy from one which is dominantly agricultural to one

containing a growing industrial sector. In the search for an all-embracing theory, Mellor identifies three interrelated segments: first, covering the role of agriculture in economic development; second, the economic nature of premodernized agriculture; and finally, the economic process of the modernization path. Because agriculture is, by its very nature, an industry of substantial relative proportion at the start of any early development, initial development itself is a process of modernization rather than the creation of a new industry (Mellor, 1967).

Mellor suggests that agricultural production conditions vary so greatly both between different countries and within single countries—as indeed they do within Brazil—that the type of product which can be produced in any one area, the kinds of resources available for production and the transformation between input and output will vary accordingly. During the development process there will be an inevitable decline in agriculture as a result of increasing specialization in production which transfers many non-agricultural jobs from the farm household to the urban centers, and lower elasticities of demand for agricultural products—as compared to non-agricultural—as incomes rise. In addition, geographic differences and high transport costs prevent extreme specialization within agriculture.

There are several points of interaction between the farm and non-farm sectors during the economic transformation (Mellor, 1967). Foremost is the major relative shift of labor between the sectors, with the consequent problem of providing food supplies to the growing urban sector; second, the growth of the urban sector requires considerable capital injection (and agriculture is for the most part a major source of this capital); third, the large, remaining agricultural sector can provide the vital markets for the products of the growing industrial base; and finally, a highly productive agriculture is dependent on much of its inputs originating outside the agricultural sector.

The starting point for much of development theory is therefore the concept of the dual economy. The dual economy approach is based on efforts to understand the relationships between the traditional sector and the growing modern sector in developing economies. Much of the early theory was based on the concept of static dualism. Later work, of which undoubtedly its most well known proponent is W. A. Lewis (1954, 1979) took account of the dynamic nature of the relationship between the two sectors, and a series of models were developed based on the concept of dynamic dualism. The basis of Lewis's analysis is an economic system with three major characteristics: a two sector economy, modern and the other traditional; unskilled labor is paid more in the modern than in the traditional sector for the same effort; and unskilled labor is initially abundant, inasmuch as the traditional sector has more labor on offer than the modern sector would wish to absorb.

Lewis points out how the expansion of the modern sector may benefit the traditional sector in several ways, each of which has its loss counterpart. These ways include the provision of employment, the sharing of physical facilities, the modernization of ideas and institutions, and trade.

Much of the relationship between the modern and the traditional sectors depends on the degree of population pressure. Where the population is scarce, the modern sector is frequently a predator, while on the other extreme where the population is dense, the modern sector "throws a life line" to the traditional sector (Lewis, 1979). In the latter case, people pour out of the traditional sector faster than the modern sector can absorb them, with unemployment rising in urban areas no matter how rapidly industrial sector employment may increase.

The expansion of the modern sector entails the construction of a physical infrastructure including highways, railroads, and port facilities, which also benefit the traditional sector. In addition, the creation and modernization of ideas in the modern sector impact, according to Lewis, on the traditional in the form of better health, education, cooperative institutions, and possibly improved land tenure systems. However, Lewis does not fail to point out that many of the "new ideas" might not be appropriate, resulting in features such as inappropriate technology. The final mutual benefit between the two sectors is trade. This might simply be trade between the sectors or the benefits from export of part of any surplus, facilitating the import of capital or consumption goods to the modern sector. This accounts for the scope of import substitution in the post-World War II years (Lewis, 1979).

The partial dependence of the modern sector upon the traditional for its needs for continued expansion will depend on a similar expansion of production within the traditional sector. Otherwise the terms of trade will move against it. Further work on the dual economy concept produced a series of growth models based on Lewis's early work. Notable among these was the work of Ranis and Fei (1964). Developed from the early work of Lewis, G. Ranis and J. C. Fei's model is based on the characteristics of the traditional or subsistence sector which are, fundamentally, high rates of population growth with a labor surplus containing widespread underemployment or disguised underemployment, and a marginal productivity of labor of zero. Agriculture, in the Ranis and Fei model, contributes both workers and surplus production to the expansion of the modern sector. In such a system, the major directions of public policy will be to design institutions which transfer the ownership of the surpluses in the traditional sector to the government or entrepreneurs in the expanding modern sector. As with the Lewis model, the continuing expansion of the traditional sector is crucial. The critical point is that at which the marginal product of labor rises above zero. At this stage the release of further labor from the traditional sector does not release a sufficient surplus to support the transfer to the modern sector, resulting in the terms of trade turning against the industrial sector. The Ranis and Fei model substantiates the implication that any shift in the domestic terms of trade toward agriculture will act as a break on economic transformation which can only be offset by some combination of technological change in agriculture and a slowdown of population growth (Hyami and Ruttan, 1971).

The assumption of underemployment or disguised unemployment in the traditional sector has been the basis for a great deal of controversy. Although ruled out by the neoclassical theorists, the concept of the traditional sector being able to yield labor without loss of output has been in the literature for many years. Folke Dovring has suggested that there are many ways of looking at the question and underscores the significance of the issue (1979). Theodore Schultz severely questions the concept, and provides several examples of dramatic losses in output through the removal of sections of the labor force in the traditional sector. One of the examples he cites was in Belo Horizonte in Brazil, where an upsurge in construction drew workers from the nearby countryside; agricultural production fell as a consequence. The reduction in output led Schultz to reject the disguised unemployment hypothesis (1964), however, Schultz's examples have been open to much criticism; the weakness is largely is in the empirical data and the particular seasons or areas involved (Ghatak and Ingersent, 1984, 58). Schultz also puts great emphasis on the investment in human capital in the traditional sector and the potential benefits of improving the quality of human resources in agriculture, arguing that human capital is a major source of economic growth (1964, 176).

Michael Todaro takes a different approach, based on the view that the modern sector requires factors other than a constant supply of labor including capital and skills. These factors often are in scarce supply. Todaro's model of labor migration and urban unemployment demonstrates why there could be a continual existence of rural-urban migration even in the face of urban unemployment, and that this migration in fact often represents a rational economic decision from the individual's point of view (1959). Hence important policy objectives might be to reduce the level of out-migration from the traditional sector to contain the number of urban unemployed by expanding agriculture.

Yet another proponent of the theory of surplus manpower in the agricultural sector was Raul Prebisch. He maintained that only a part of the economically active population was productively absorbed; a very high proportion constituted redundant manpower in rural areas (1950). Where the manpower surplus remained large, migrants from rural areas simply shifted the scene of their redundancy. Prebisch emphasized the fact that the broad masses of Latin America's rural population, formally cut off by the illiteracy which had debarred them from access to books and newspapers, were swiftly becoming receptive to modern communications and increasing the need to speed the rate of development. He also asked whether more people could have been retained within agriculture had agricultural development been faster and so relieved the congestion in the cities. He blamed a number of factors, including the slow rate of growth of domestic and external demand, outdated marketing systems, price policies, the system of land tenure, and the use and inadequacy of technical progress; and pointed out that the majority of increases in production in Latin America had been as a result of bringing new land into cultivation.

Perhaps the most influential theories on the failure of Latin American countries to achieve acceptable growth rates and diminish their dependence on the developed economies came during the post-World War II period from the advocates of the center-periphery thesis, the leading proponent of which was Prebisch. The argument rested on the theory that the slow rate of development by the less-developed nations was as much a result of their historic relationship with the developed nations as of internal imbalances (Prebisch, 1950).

Under the traditional patterns of the international division of labor, the specific role of the Latin American countries was to produce food and raw materials for the great industrial centers. There was no place within this schema for the industrialization of new countries. Prebisch's original theory was written in the immediate post-World War II period, after the world had been through two world wars and a major economic crisis. He maintained that the economic advantages of the international division of labor, although theoretically sound, were based on assumptions that had been conclusively proved false by the facts. He argued that the enormous benefits accruing from increases in productivity did not reach the periphery in a measure comparable to that obtained by the peoples of the great industrial centers. This accounts for the outstanding differences between the standard of living of the former and the latter, and their respective abilities to accumulate capital. His reasoning included the argument that the international terms of trade for products from the periphery would continually worsen in favor of the center. The solution lay in domestic industrial expansion (Prebisch, 1970).

The general support the Prebisch argument received among Latin American countries, particularly Brazil, led the way in a sustained drive toward forced industrialization during a period of import substitution with heavily protected internal expansion. Prebisch maintained that primary exports should not be sacrificed to further industrialization, because they were needed not only to generate foreign exchange to purchase new capital goods, but also because their value included a high proportion of land rent which involved no collective cost. In the event, as mentioned in Chapter 1, the need to finance industrial expansion, plus the desire to maintain the low cost of wage goods eventually drove Brazilian agriculture into a severe crisis.

The theory of unequal exchange between the center and the periphery was extended by Alain de Janvry. He discounts the introduction of new technology as a panacea to deal with the ills of rural poverty (1975). His argument was that underdevelopment cannot be treated apart from development if less advanced areas are related by the market to developed economies. In addition this should be examined against a background of historical events that had been dominated by the nature of accumulation in more developed countries. He felt, as did Prebisch, that the concepts of periphery and marginality are essential for the construction of a theory of underdevelopment. The concept of the marginals would be reflected in Brazil by the "minifundistas."

De Janvry emphasized that the historical transformation of Latin America as a periphery of the developed center occurred first through colonization, and later through selfish interests of powerful, developed nations. Furthermore, de Janvry maintained, policies encouraged the maintenance of economic systems based on trade in primary products against manufactured goods and hence provided the basis for class alliances between the traditional landed elite and international capitalists. This allowed the former to "capture a significant part of the surplus from the export of agricultural products and to enjoy consumption patterns similar to those in developed countries" (de Janvry, 1975). Under this system, the traditional land owners were able to retain the advantages that had been theirs historically, such as cheap labor, and social and political power. This set in motion an economic system in which the traditional landowners extended their control toward industry and finance while retaining control of the land. Hence they were able to maintain their influence on the political system, and in particular, use their influence to maintain a balance of economic advantage weighted in their favor.

With the advent of import substitution industrialization, a new dynamism was injected into the industrial sector. However, this tended to depress the internal terms of trade against wage goods, creating a situation where "profitable investment ventures were confined to a subset of the industrial sector which was oriented to satisfy the demand of the upper classes" (de Janvry, 1975). This in itself led to increasing demand for advanced technology and imported capital goods, and eventually to foreign exchange problems. By the 1960s, the modern sector had become an enclave of industrialization which was unable to generate sufficient employment to absorb the available labor. In this linkage, between the export sector of primary products and the import sector of capital goods for the production of luxury consumption items, de Janvry concluded lay the rationale of labor incorporation in the central developed economies and marginality in the peripheral areas (de Janvry, 1975).

The attacks on the "classical theory" of international trade which, as already discussed, was held to be unfavorable to the economic development of the less-developed countries, was in turn criticized by H. Myint. Myint argued strongly that there are elements in the classical theory which are applicable and can be utilized to the general benefit of developing nations. Basing his analysis of classical theory largely on Adam Smith's The Wealth of Nations, Myint distills two fundamental principles of importance. First, international trade overcomes the constraints of the domestic market and provides an outlet for products which are surplus to this market. This Myint terms the "vent for surplus" theory of international trade. Second, Myint argues, by widening the extent of the market, international trade does improve the division of labor and increases the general level of productivity within the country. This he calls the "productivity" theory (Myint, 1958). It is the first of these points which appears most relevant to the situation Brazil found itself in after the first bout of import substitution industrialization in the 1960s.

Myint contrasts the "vent for surplus" theory with the "comparative cost" argument (Myint, 1958). The latter, he asserts, assumes that the resources of a country are given and are fully employed before it enters into international trade. The function of international trade is thus to reallocate the given resources more efficiently between domestic and export production. In contrast, the "vent for surplus" theory assumes that the country about to enter into international trade possesses some surplus productive capacity and that part of its resource base would have remained unused had it not been for international trade. Export production can therefore be increased with no reduction in domestic production (Myint, 1958). This concept obviously implies an inelastic domestic demand for the exportable commodity. There is, therefore, no conflict between the benefits to the domestic and the export economy, and a large element of the resource utilized in the production of the export good is in fact costless. In the Brazilian situation the "costless" resource is uncultivated land and, in the context of this discussion, the surplus product is soybeans, a product which without exports has only a very limited market.

Myint emphasizes Adam Smith's conjecture that the extent of the home market is allied to the level of economic organization within a country. The concept of surplus land implies a combination with surplus labor. This labor being regarded as "unproductive" and should not be confused with "disguised unemployment" which is associated with shortages of land and high rural populations (Myint, 1958).

The failure to capitalize upon this potential, such as Myint suggests, by giving too little attention to the agricultural export sector and diverting too much capital and technical resources to industrial development projects would eventually considerably reduce foreign exchange earning potential so urgently needed for economic development.

THE EFFECTIVENESS OF THE BRAZILIAN APPROACH

Several authors have examined the impact of contemporary Brazilian agricultural development upon the general development of Brazil. An early study, and one of the first to use empirical data, was made by William Nicholls in the late 1960s (1969). The study traces the early development of Brazil, and specifically examines the interrelationships between the developing industrial-urban complex and agriculture in the state of Sao Paulo during the years 1940-1950 and the policy developments in Brazil in the subsequent decade. Nicholls concluded that by facilitating the flow of capital into agriculture and by absorbing part of the rural labor force, the local industrial development in Sao Paulo had had a substantial influence in raising productivity and incomes of farmers in the surrounding area. Local agriculture obtained significant benefits, particularly from the urban-oriented infrastructure which grew up and spilled over into rural areas.

The study goes on, however, to severely criticize the generally unfavorable effects on employment caused by the encouragement of capital intensive industries, the efforts of the government to maintain low wages, and the heavy import subsidies which encouraged excessive levels of mechanization. Furthermore, found the benefits to the remainder of the country were harder to ascertain, although there were benefits from the considerable expansion of communication-- particularly the highway system--and hence a move toward some generalization of market opportunities.

On the other hand, in a later work, Peter Knight found that there had been a notable failure to introduce many aspects of modern agricultural technology to regions other than those immediately adjacent to the new urban centers. The projections of import demand growth in the late 1960s were already pointing toward an increasing need for foreign exchange. Although there was, in the late 1960s, considerable potential for rapid increases in productivity in the agricultural sector in the South, for this to be accomplished, let alone the more ambitious objectives of greater sectorial and regional equity, would require a far greater political commitment (1971).

Other authors have examined Brazilian policy objectives, initiatives, and achievements in the agricultural sector during the same period, notably Gordon Smith (1969) and Nicholls (1972). Smith found that specific objectives were often confused, and agricultural policy initiatives--in particular the impact of pre-announced minimum prices--often achieved perverse results. Both studies found that the dominant factor in the 1960s was the Brazilian government's desire to encourage industrialization at the expense of agriculture. Nicholls stressed the enormous contribution of the Brazilian highway system in opening up markets throughout the nation for consumer goods and providing access to urban centers for agricultural produce (1969).

A further benchmark study of the period leading up to 1970 was made by G. Edward Schuh (1970). This detailed account of the development of Brazilian agriculture empha- sized the imbalances within agriculture rather than its failure to contribute to economic growth. Specifically singled out was lack of investment, firstly in research and secondly in "people," and the fact that the research system was low in relation to the needs of the country. It was suggested that the substantial potential for strengthening Brazil's position in the world market, given its rich endowment of agricultural resources, should continue to provide a valuable source of exchange earnings in addition to providing food at lower prices for the domestic market. Much, Schuh argued, depended on greater investment in human capital. Formal education available to rural people was well below that of their urban counterparts, and the consequences were, the study maintained, "pervasive. Little innovative activity takes place among large fractions of the rural population, little attempt is made to adopt new ways of doing things. Hence, much of the agricultural sector remains tradition-bound" (Schuh, 1970).

More recently, several studies have been made by Fernando Homen de Melo (1978, 1983). One study examined the effects of Brazilian policy in the postwar period, looking particularly at the repercussions they had had on the agricultural sector. Homem de Melo pointed out that as recently as the beginning of the last war, nearly 70 percent of Brazil's working population was still employed in the primary sector. Such industrialization as had taken place prior to the end of World War II had been as a result of external circumstances and the domestic market's natural growth, rather than from any initiative on the part of the Brazilian government. Subsequently once again much of the initiative was as a result of internal and external press- ures. The Homem de Melo study draws attention to the emergence of the soybean crop in the 1960s and the early stages of its rapid expansion (1978). By the mid-1970s the situation faced by the Brazilian economy was, and has remained, the dual pressure of the critical need to maintain the balance of payments and earn foreign exchange, and also to deal with domestic supply, taking into account food price trends and their distributive consequences.

Homem de Melo argued that Brazil's foreign earnings were heavily dependent on outside events, in particular on high international prices for agricultural commodities (1978). In the 1970s concern about the distributive aspects of development in Brazil began to grow. Substantial gains were being made in the developed South; favorable international prices and the available technology was showing up in the continued expansion of soybeans and at that time had, according to Homem de Melo, the greatest short-run potential. In contrast, domestic products were showing little evidence of productivity increases, and this pointed towards future problems (1983). The double pressures of the balance of payments disequilibrium, which meant a continuing need to increase exports but on the other hand provided an inadequate supply to the domestic market largely due to prices, manifested itself in nutrition problems for low-income families and "probably explains why foreign exchange policies were not put to more radical use as a solution to the balance of payments problem" (Homem de Melo, 1983).

This argument was substantiated by Gary Williams and R. L. Thompson (1984) who concluded that clashing policy directives in the 1970s actually restricted the growth of soybean production, offsetting the stimulative effects of intervention in the soybean oil and meal markets, and therefore preventing the attainment of the very objectives for which the intervention had been undertaken. The problem of conflicting policy objectives is again referred to in a World Bank study (1979a).

The serious distributive consequences of some of the Brazilian government's agricultural policy approaches has been dealt with by Fox (1979) in a study on the Northeast, and--in relation to food policy and its consequences for consumption--by Cheryl Grey (1982). Fox examines one policy instrument, the fixing of minimum prices, and looks at its impact on agriculture in the Northeast. He deals with the very different circumstances that are faced by farmers in the Brazilian Northeast and throws some doubt upon the efficacy of the policy to deal with them. (Fox, 1979). The Grey study is concerned with the nutritional implications of Brazilian food policy and underscores the immense problems which still exist in terms of malnutrition in Brazil. Grey points out that as recently as 1975 more than half Brazil's children suffered some degree of malnourishment. Highly significant is the fact that the major problem is inadequate calorie intake. The study found that the poor in Brazil have more protein in their diet than the poor in many developing countries. However, Grey suggests, as many as 30 million individuals suffer from a deficiency in calorie intake (1982).

3
Brazilian Agricultural Policy

SETTING THE SCENE--AGRICULTURAL POLICY BACKGROUND

Post World War II Until the 1960s

Since the end of World War II, the attitude of successive
Brazilian governments toward agriculture and their consequent
policy initiatives falls into two quite distinct phases. The
first period, dating from the end of the war until the early
1960s, reflected the predominant feeling among Brazilian
policy makers of the time that, as suggested in Chapter 1,
most of the difficulties facing the economy had been a result
of Brazil's dependence on outside forces which during the
depressed interwar years had left Brazil at the mercy of the
developed industrial economies. They were no doubt much
influenced by the then very fashionable "import substitution
school of thought," articulated by Prebisch in the early
1950s. This suggested that developing countries should make
positive moves to exert their independence from world markets
(which were considered to be dominated by the rich countries)
by engaging in import substitution industrialization (ISI).

As a result Brazilian agriculture went through a period
of extensive neglect--even to a degree, practical discrim-
ination--as all attention was placed on spurring industrial
growth and maintaining low consumer food prices. In spite of
this, however, the overall growth of the agricultural sector
during this period was not unimpressive, as Table 3-1
implies.

Table 3-1   Indexes of Total Output of Principal Crops:
Brazil, 1948-67
(1948-52 = 100)

Crop	1948-52	1953-57	1958-62	1963-67
Beans	100	122	135	180
Corn	100	118	146	193
Rice	100	122	163	222
Wheat	100	177	128	117
Cassava	100	118	139	197
Potatoes	100	130	153	185
Peanuts	100	127	336	504
Cotton	100	102	135	159
Bananas	100	130	162	219
Oranges	100	109	137	185
Sugar	100	129	173	219
Tobacco	100	126	144	202
Cacao	100	127	130	133
Coffee	100	110	191	132
Principal Crops	100	118	157	182

Source: Adapted from Nicholls, 1972.

Even growing at a rate of half that of the industrial
sector, growth in output per capita remained positive. It
should be noted that little of this growth came from technical improvement; virtually all was a result of bringing
more land under cultivation, and much was through further
exploitation of the frontier.   This period, as already
suggested above, lasted until a series of factors caused a
rise in food prices toward the end of the 1950s, culminating
in a supply crisis in the early 1960s.   The supply crisis
pushed prices up faster than the level of inflation and
brought in its wake both social and political unrest. This
eventually led to the collapse of the democratic government,
which was replaced by a military regime in 1964.   The food
crisis brought to the surface doubts regarding the validity
of theories behind the continuing neglect of agriculture and
the relevance of total dependence on the import substitution
philosophy. With this, in the early 1960s, came a positive
rethinking of the role of agriculture in the developing
Brazilian economy (Nicholls, 1971).

Until that point, the central objective of Brazilian economic policy had been almost entirely devoted to the support of industrial development. In essence, the support for industrial growth was based on a three-pronged program: protection against international competition, easy access of industry to capital, and stable wages. Therefore, the role of agriculture was to produce food at prices deemed acceptable to the urban wage earner. A secondary function was the generation of foreign exchange to make possible the importation of capital goods and industrial raw materials. This was to be achieved by an "exportable surplus" derived, at the time, almost entirely from coffee, which was subjected to substantial export taxes. As suggested above, during the period 1953-1957 there was also a system of multiple exchange rates which heavily discriminated against agriculture and intentionally held down farm product prices.

Agriculture was not to be regarded as a vital growth sector but as a "reservoir for surplus labor" not absorbed in the rapid industrialization process (Nicholls, 1971). The rationale behind this view came from the assumed lack of growth potential for agricultural products, caused by the traditionally low-income elasticities of demand, both in the domestic, and the international markets. This was the substance of the Prebisch thesis. There was also some indication that Brazilian policy makers believed that rapid industrialization was the most direct route to a position of world stature for Brazil—a view that still holds—and this was seen as overriding the need for a more traditional process as might have been more applicable to the rural areas of Brazil, which still contained in excess of 40 percent of the population.

In addition to the discrimination against agriculture in the drive for industrialization, rural areas also suffered from chronic neglect of education, agricultural research and extension (Smith, 1969). Nevertheless, agriculture was able, to expand apace. Probably the most tangible albeit indirect aid to agriculture at the time, was a result of the considerable public investment into the expansion of the Brazilian highways system. The total road network grew from 302,147 km to 803,068 km between 1952 and 1965 (Smith, 1969). Until then the very limited access to the interior had made producers heavily dependent on proximity to markets near the coast. The improvement of transportation, both for produce and people, aided by the very low absorption of labor in industry, permitted a considerable amount of new lands to be opened up. Whatever the net impact other aspects of public

policy may have had, directly or indirectly, upon agricultural investment in the 1950s, their contribution was
dwarfed by the benefits to agriculture of the Brazilian
highway construction program. Indeed, most of the growth in
output during the decade 1950–1960 can be attributed to the
stimulus to development at the frontier through the improvement to transportation (Nicholls, 1972).

The first direct policy initiative was a minimum price
program, first enacted in 1943 but not initiated until 1951.
During the latter part of the period there was a publicly
financed storage system, largely state-operated, which failed
through poor administration and organization to yield the
expected benefits. To partially offset the effects of the
multiple exchange rate system, which was detrimental to farm
returns at the time, Brazilian farmers did for some time
benefit from favorable rates of exchange on some of their
major inputs, particularly tractors, fuel, fertilizers, and
heavy trucks. Fertilizer import subsidies, which effectively
reduced the domestic price by half relative to crop prices,
helped to increase substantially the use of fertilizers.
However, such benefits were unequal in their distribution,
both between farms and between regions, the proportion of
farmers who actually used these inputs being so small
(Nicholls, 1972).

It was recognized quite early on that one of the
greatest problems facing agriculture was the shortage of
credit. The very low priority agriculture received in this
sphere is illustrated by the small proportion of funds
allocated to agriculture by the Brazilian Development Bank in
its first decade of operation. Between 1952 and 1962 only 4
percent of the local currency loans went to the agricultural
sector (Baer, 1983). However, there is some doubt about the
assumption that, in terms of credit, the neglect of agriculture is valid. Agricultural credit as a proportion of the
sectors' output and as a proportion to total credit grew
slightly during the period, while in the same period commercial and industrial credit declined as a share of those
sectors' products (Tendler, 1969).

Brazil's public policy throughout the 1950s therefore
had been primarily concerned with the exploitation of
agriculture to finance Brazil's industrial growth rather than
the promotion of rural welfare or agricultural output. There
were exceptions to this rule, however; the wheat support
policy was the one example of an ISI policy being applied to
an agricultural product, and there was continuing attention
paid to Brazil's main export crop, coffee. The minimum price

policy, referred to above, had been on the statute book since 1943 but as yet had played virtually no part in spite of attempts to reactivate it in 1951. For these reasons the period must be regarded as a time of relative stagnation in Brazilian agriculture.

1960 to 1980: Crisis, then Expansion

The 1960s saw increasing pressure on the traditionally inefficient Brazilian agricultural sector. A series of poor harvests compounded with years of neglect resulted in a sudden rise in food prices and severe supply shortages in urban centers. Food price rises contributed to inflation which was rising faster than the minimum wage, and severe political pressure combined with social unrest resulted in inept efforts to combat price increases by administrative controls. There were frequent attempts at short-term adjustments in the hope of increasing food availability and reducing tension in urban areas, but this had very little effect on long-term growth in agriculture. The government had manifestly failed to get a grip on the fundamental problems which had faced Brazilian agriculture since the end of the war, and by 1962-1963 the situation had reached crisis proportions. An obvious and urgent need for a new political initiative toward agriculture became obvious.

The food crisis initially led the government to take further steps to obtain short-term increases in production while attempting to hold down prices in the urban centers. However, there was already evidence that by 1961 the government had begun to reassess the role agriculture might play in the Brazilian economy. The first positive steps were taken to make the price guarantee scheme more effective and the wheat support scheme was reorganized, but the concentration on rural credit as the main impetus underpinning the drive for expansion of agricultural output took precedence over all other areas of Brazilian agriculture. There began to be greater efforts to improve research and extension, and the government began to consider some positive action to achieve an improved land tenure system and a consequent redistribution of land.

POLICY INSTRUMENTS

The Minimum Price Program

Background

The minimum price program was the first, and remains the most comprehensive, attempt by Brazilian policy makers to use direct methods to influence farmers' planting decisions. The intention was to reduce the uncertainties facing farmers at the beginning of the planting season and thus encourage higher levels of production and investment. This was to be achieved by, first, providing farmers with a guaranteed market for their products at prices which would at least cover their costs of production and, second, providing the minimum prices as a guide to planting choices. In addition, the program was linked to a credit scheme based on loans against the value of the crops covered by the policy. It was launched initially in 1943 through the creation of a federal agency exclusively concerned with price policies in agriculture. This was the Production Finance Commission (CFP), which came under the jurisdiction of the Ministry of Finance. This agency could design financial plans for agricultural production in the "interests of the economy and military defence of the nation." However, the execution of these plans required approval of the government (Duran, 1979). The first minimum prices were announced for the 1945-1946 harvest year for rice, black beans, corn, soybeans, and sunflower seeds. In the early years of the scheme the actual minimum prices levels were legislated, and the commission had only theoretical responsibility for approving the cultivated area to which these minimum prices were to be applied. In any event, the minimum price levels were set so low as to have no practical effect.

It was not until 1951 that new legislation was passed which gave the commission itself the power to set the minimum price levels. In addition, for the first time, the legislation specified the beneficiaries of the policy. Prices were set for cereals and other domestic crops, with preference to producers and their cooperatives (Duran, 1979). Which groups were actually to benefit from minimum price support remained a matter of considerable debate. Subsequent legislation exemplified the immense difficulties that have dogged Brazilian agricultural support schemes in their attempts to ensure that the support actually went to the producers as originally intended. A further objective of the minimum price policy and its associated storage schemes was to smooth out the sharp fluctuations to which crop prices are subject during the course of the crop year. However, between 1951 and 1961, one of the main problems surrounding the policy was the lack of public storage for the crops that had been financed. This was shown in a 1962 study which demonstrated that 99 percent of the credit provided under the minimum price scheme for acquisitions by the government went, in fact, to millers and exporters rather than to farmers (Nicholls, 1972).

Regardless, the price levels were set so low that their impact proved negligible during the 1950s and early 1960s (Smith, 1969). The attitude of the government was half-hearted, and prices were only announced after the completion of planting, which defeated one of the fundamental objectives of the scheme. This was yet a further demonstration of the general neglect of agriculture because the problems of the agricultural sector were not felt of sufficient importance to warrant the risk of higher food and raw material prices which might have risked the central objective of industrial growth. The situation was to change completely when food prices started to rise in the late 1950s, culminating in the supply crisis in 1962. Agriculture was suddenly regarded as a "bottleneck sector" (Nicholls, 1979), and from then on an effective increase in output was regarded as a high priority.

The 1963 Plano Triennial saw land reform as a basic solution, but the government chose the alternatives of substantially expanding rural credit and reactivating the minimum price program (Smith, 1969). Between 1962 and 1964, several schemes were devised to exclude millers and exporters from the minimum price program, with hope that farmers would obtain a more substantial part of the available credit under the policy. Legislation passed in 1962 specified that marketing credit was only to be available to farmers and their cooperatives, but millers and exporters could partake in the scheme until the end of 1963. Later this was extended to 1965, allowing them the possibility of obtaining credit for raw materials, providing they could prove they had paid farmers the minimum prices under the policy. Later, when the military government took over in 1964, millers, exporters and agribusinesses were included on a permanent basis. During this period the scope of the scheme was extended and prices indexed for the first time. The available credit under the policy was extended from 60 to 100 percent of the quoted minimum price, and interest on loans was charged on the basis of the length of time the loan had been taken up, rather than the period specified in the contract. The idea behind this was to emphasize the credit side rather than the acquisition side of the policy. This encouraged farmers to seek better prices after harvest rather than selling the crop to the government at the quoted minimum price at harvest (Duran, 1979).

In 1967 the scheme was again modified; first, by transferring the commission--while leaving its administrative autonomy intact--from the Ministry of Finance to the Ministry of Agriculture; second, by fixing minimum prices within specific area of each state to be announced net; and third prices were to be announced at least three months prior to the planting period. The general objective of these modifications was to give the scheme a long-run role, to replace its previously short-run influence to the current year's prices.

Operation

The operation of the minimum price program gave the producer or cooperative the option of selling such crops as fell within the minimum price program either to the market at the going price or to the CFP at the guaranteed minimum price, or borrowing against the minimum price value of the stored crop for later sale either to the market or to the government (i.e. raising credit against the security of the crop). As we have said, after 1967, millers and exporters could also participate in the scheme, provided they had initially paid the producer the minimum price.

The operation of the sales option was under the Federal Government Acquisition Scheme (AGF) and the storage option was under the Federal Government loans program (EGF). There were two types of EGF loan. One was a loan without the option to sell the crop to the government; in this case the farmer was able to borrow up to 80 percent of the value of the crop at the minimum price for a period of 120 days. The crop remained in the farmer's storage and at the end of the period the loan had to be repaid along with all financial costs, whatever the market price at the time. The second type gave the borrower the option to sell the crop to the government. In the latter case the loan could be up to 100 percent of the value of the crop at the minimum price, for a period which varies from 90 to 300 days.

Should the market price rise above the minimum at any time during the loan period, the borrower could sell to the market and repay the government plus all the costs involved; should the price remain below the minimum, then the crop had to be sold to the government at the minimum price and the loan repaid out of the proceeds, with the government bearing all the costs. In that case, the storage was to be in warehouses approved by the Banco do Brasil. A variant of the latter scheme was the rural promissory note which, when discounted, allowed for credit in excess of the minimum price with, however, an added requirement that repayments were made during the period of the loan. This scheme provided finance at a level theoretically more in line with market prices. Soybean growers were major users of this option (Duran, 1979).

Impact
    Any analysis of the workings of the minimum price program is complicated by the twin elements within the program: the minimum prices themselves as guide to planting, and the loan programs associated with the minimum price program. For the period 1962-1966, support prices for domestic staples such as rice, corn and beans were somewhat erratic inasmuch as prices were changed annually, apparently as a function of the internal market price at the time of planting. The higher the real market price, the higher the support price, suggesting that the support was provided according to production in each particular year. This meant that the support prices were high when the market was high and low when it was low, thus providing farmers with no additional guide other than the market (Smith, 1969, 246). It is not hard to conclude that farmers were ready to look either for crops with a more stable price history within the domestic market or for incentives outside the domestic market which might provide them with a greater degree of perceived stability.
    More substantial analyses of the impact of the minimum price policy upon farmers' production planning were conducted by Smith for the period to 1966, and by Duran for the period 1968-1976. They showed that the preannounced prices probably had no influence upon farmers' planting intentions with respect to domestic crops. However, the conclusion concerning cotton in the first study and cotton and soybeans in the second stated that the minimum price guide was accepted as a good proxy for expected prices leading to a reduction in the uncertainty factor. This in turn could have brought about reductions in the planting of domestic crops which were unwanted in terms of the stated aims of the policy (Duran, 1979).
    Take up of credit under the scheme shows substantial variations between crops, between regions, and between groups. Table 3-2 shows the relative shares of the benefi- ciaries of credit under the minimum price policy between the years 1967-68 and 1975-76. In terms of development, the

breakdown between the North and Northeast and the remainder of the country is noteworthy, as is the division between producers and non-producers. In the Center-South the situation favored farmers; the reverse was the case in the North-Northeast. Table 3-3 shows the regional distribution, and Table 3-4 indicates the proportion of this credit that was diverted to one crop, soybeans.

Table 3-2 Relative Shares of the Beneficiaries of Credit under the Minimum Price Policy according to Region 1967/68 to 1975/76 (%)

Region	1967-68	1969-70	1971-72	1973-74	1975-76
Center-South: Producers and Cooperatives	57.0	64.0	53.0	52.0	68.0
Others[1]	43.0	36.0	47.0	48.0	32.0
	100.0	100.0	100.0	100.0	100.0
North-Northeast: Producers and Cooperatives	9.0	20.0	10.0	11.0	32.0
Others[1]	91.0	80.0	90.0	89.0	68.0
	100.0	100.0	100.0	100.0	100.0
Brazil: Producers and Cooperatives	44.0	59.0	48.0	46.0	63.0
Others[1]	56.0	42.0	42.0	54.0	37.0
	100.0	100.0	100.0	100.0	100.0

[1] Others include Millers, Exporters, and Agroindustries.
Source: Adapted from Duran, 1979.

Table 3-3   Geographical Distribution of Credit under the
     Minimum Price Policy, 1967/68 to 1975/76
              (millions of current cruzeiros)

Region	1967-68	1969-70	1971-72	1973-74	1975-76
Center-South	153	343	876	2,426	10,129
Share (%)	73.0	88.0	88.0	85.0	86.0
North-Northeast	56	46	114	423	1,666
Share (%)	27.0	12.0	12.0	15.0	14.0
Brazil	209	389	990	2,849	11,795

Source: Adapted from Duran, 1979.

Table 3-4   Soybeans: Relative Shares of Production Financed
     under the Minimum Price Policy of Total Production in
           Selected States, 1967/68 to 1975/76 (%)

State	1967-68	1969-70	1971-72	1973-74	1975-76
Sao Paulo	54.0	30.0	27.0	39.0	28.0
Parana	12.0	13.0	27.0	25.0	43.0
Santa Caterina	27.0	19.0	29.0	18.0	30.0
Rio Grande do Sul	10.0	12.0	16.0	14.0	28.0
Brazil	13.0	19.0	20.0	19.0	29.0

Source: Adapted from Duran, 1979.

General Rural Credit

Background
     Rural credit, for the most part at heavily subsidized
real rates of interest, has been the backbone of Brazilian
agricultural support policies not only as a fundamental part
of the minimum price program, but also in its own right as
direct policy. Whereas in the 1950s it was estimated that
only 18 percent of the total credit utilized by agriculture
came from institutional sources, with most of the remainder
coming from merchants, processors, or private sources (Smith,
1969), the 1960s saw substantial increases ˙from the institutional sector. It has been estimated that the real value of
agricultural loans increased by a multiple of six, and the

ratio of agricultural credit to total credit increased from
11 percent in 1960 to virtually 25 percent by the mid-1970s.

The origins of the rural credit policy lay in the widely
held belief that lack of credit--or lack of access to capital
--was responsible not only for the depressing effect upon
farm product prices, such as the traditional problems of
farmers being dependent upon middle men and being forced to
sell at harvest through inability to finance storage, but
also for inhibiting investment and expansion in agriculture,
particularly in domestic food crops.

The Rural Credit policy was established with the
following central objectives:

1. To facilitate the supply of capital to farmers,
   especially those with medium or small-sized holdings.
2. To encourage and facilitate the introduction of
   new production techniques.
3. To encourage the purchase of modern inputs.

Table 3-5   Indicators of Agricultural Credit, 1960-74

Year	Agr. Credit ———————— Agr. Output	(%)	Agr. Credit ———————— Total Credit
1960	15.20		10.21
1961	16.90		9.96
1962	15.89		9.35
1963	19.34		10.89
1964	19.55		10.96
1965	22.06		10.51
1966	20.14		13.42
1967	21.05		14.41
1968	22.39		20.78
1969	28.87		25.98
1970	36.62		26.54
1971	36.61		26.97
1972	38.78		27.44
1973	40.15		27.72
1974	41.75		29.40

Source: Homem de Melo, 1983.

Although agricultural credit historically has been
regarded as a low priority, total credit to agriculture did
grow significantly during the period (see Table 3-5), but it

was not until after the later 1960s and the early 1970s that it showed very substantial growth, averaging 18.5 percent per year in real terms (see Table 3-6). In 1975, the total flow of agricultural credit actually exceeded the net agricultural output. The growth of longer term investment credits was particularly rapid. By the end of the 1970s it was suggested in a survey by the Banco do Brasil that some 31 percent of Brazilian farmers were being reached by the formal credit system (World Bank, 1979a, 16-17).

Table 3-6   Growth of Agricultural Output and Total
                   Credit Flows to Agriculture, 1969-70

(1969=100)

Year	Net Value of Agric. Output	Crop Credits	Livestock Credits	Total	Total Credit Flow as % of Net Value of Output
1969	100	100	100	100	45
1970	100	124	107	119	54
1971	116	143	125	137	54
1972	126	178	153	170	61
1973	159	245	230	241	69
1974	183	312	266	298	74
1975	191	445	410	434	102
1976	213	462	408	445	95
1977	256	450	281	397	70
1978	250	430	347	404	73
1979	268	532	439	503	85

Source: World Bank, 1979a.

Operation
    Credit, including that supplied under the minimum price program, was provided under a number of headings. The national credit system is comprised of the Banco do Brasil, the Banco Central, together with several other state and federal institutions, and the private commercial banks. Of these, the most significant is the Banco do Brasil with a share of the total agricultural lending of 65 percent in 1979. About 45 percent of credit was supplied to meet short-term production costs, with repayments varying between six months and two years; about 29 percent was advanced for long-term fixed capital, with a repayment period of five to twelve

years; and the remainder is made up of marketing credit
--falling largely within the minimum price program--and
shorter term credits for semifixed investment which were
normally repayable in two to three years.   Interest rates
were variable according to the nature and objective of the
loan. The Banco Central set the basic rates at nominal
levels.   Historically, as the rate of inflation increased so
did the relative level of subsidy to agricultural borrowers.

Table 3-7   Implicit Credit Subsidies (in Constant 1980 Cruzeiros)
                 Transferred to the Agricultural Sector through
                 the Rural Credit Portfolio, 1971-81

	Average Annual Balances (in Millions of 1980 Cruzeiros)			Credit Subsidies Transferred to Agric. Sector[1]	Agric. GDP (Millions of 1980 Cruzeiros)	Credit Subsidy/ Agric. GDP	Total Agric.Credit/ Agric. GDP
Year	Banco do Brasil	Commercial Banks	Total				
1971	157,396	90,473	247,869	11,154	424,945	2.62	58.33
1972	188,500	106,471	294,971	7,964	463,106	1.72	63.69
1973	239,926	139,378	379,304	3,431	582,783	0.59	65.08
1974	313,439	168,954	482,393	5,410	671,605	0.81	71.83
1975	447,200	208,215	655,415	6,810	703,429	0.97	93.17
1976	508,976	225,410	734,386	139,533	780,735	17.87	94.06
1977	551,506	204,598	756,104	143,660	940,883	15.27	80.36
1978	548,785	187,093	735,878	120,684	918,594	13.14	80.11
1979	545,742	152,156	697,898	168,196	985,661	17.06	70.81
1980	480,018	134,418	614,436	212,595	1,085,324	19.59	56.61
1981	385,458	117,306	502,764	155,354	1,159,126	13.40	43.37

[1]Estimated by multiplying Total lending by $(-i)$ where $i = (n - r)/1+r$, in which r is
the annual rate of inflation and n is the nominal rate of interest for Rural Credit.
Source: da Mata, 1982.

Impact
        Although the efficiency of the subsidized credit system
has been substantially questioned, its importance to Brazilian agriculture and the Brazilian economy was very significant, as Table 3-7 indicates. The level of negative
interest, and therefore the level of subsidy, although
varying from year to year, was very important over the two
decades in question, as Table 3-8 shows. It has been
suggested that farmers utilize the resources of rural credit
to supply financial markets outside the production process,
in addition to consumption and durable urban goods (Knight,
1971). Joao Sayad has suggested that nominal interest rates
are a very poor guide to planting decisions (1979). There is
little doubt that in spite of recent efforts to broaden the
base and reach more producers, over the years the distribution of credit has been heavily skewed in terms of region
(see table 3-9), crop, and landowner, with the larger landowners and specific crops getting much of the benefit.

Table 3-8   Rural Credit in Brazil, Estimated Nominal
and Real Rates of Interest, 1960-76

Year	Rate of Inflation	Interest Rate (Est. Nominal Average)	Interest Rate (Estimated Real)
1960	31	15	-16
1961	37	18	-19
1962	52	18	-34
1963	75	18	-57
1964	90	18	-72
1965	57	18	-39
1966	38	16	-22
1967	28	16	-12
1968	24	16	-8
1969	21	16	-5
1970	22	16	-6
1971	20	15	-5
1972	18	15	-3
1973	16	15	-1
1974	29	15	-14
1975	28	15	-13
1976	43	15	-28

Source: Homem de Melo, 1983, 215.

Knight also found that the granting of loans was very discriminatory in selection of type, amount, and client, with the bankers tending toward their natural banking prudence of offering short-term loans and large individual amounts to wealthier farmers (1969). A study by Flavio Quintana supported the view that the credit system was biased toward a monoculture cropping system (1982). In 1978, in Brazil as a whole, 20 percent of all crop-specific loans went to soybean producers. However, in Rio Grande do Sul in the same year, the proportion was as high as 55 percent (see Table 3-10). There is little empirical evidence available to substantiate the impact of these credit flows upon output and investment, although Sayad has questioned the conception that in an environment of low market prices subsidized credit can increase investment in agriculture to the level that would have been attained should market prices themselves have been higher, arguing that "if the rate of return in agriculture is decreased by government policies, subsidized interest rates cannot by themselves increase the rate of investment in

Table 3-9   Crop Credits to Producers and Cooperatives, by
             Type and Region, 1978 (millions of cruzeiros)

Region	Production Credit	Investment Credit	Marketing Credit	Total Crop Credit
North	1,388	1,885	457	3,730
Northeast	12,270	5,843	4,769	22,882
Southeast	30,697	8,994	17,490	57,181
South	41,260	12,245	19,580	73,085
Frontier	9,324	3,753	1,316	14,393
Total	94,939	32,720	43,612	171,271

Regional Distribution (%)

Region	Production Credit	Investment Credit	Marketing Credit	Total Crop Credit
North	1.5	5.8	1.0	2.2
Northeast	12.9	17.9	10.9	13.4
Southeast	32.3	27.5	40.1	33.4
South	43.5	37.4	44.9	42.7
Frontier	9.8	11.5	3.0	8.4
Total	100.0	100.0	100.0	100.0

Source: World Bank, 1979a.

Table 3-10   Rural Credit: Proportion of Loans According to
             Production Lines, Rio Grande do Sul, 1978 (%)

Crop	% of all loans
Rice	12.90
Potatoes	0.44
Sugar	0.04
Black Beans	0.29
Corn	3.42
Soybeans	55.00
Sorghum	0.28
Wheat	24.35
Cattle and Sheep	2.14
Other	1.14
Total	100.00

Source: Quintana, 1982.

this sector" (Sayad, 1979). Farmers will take up loans at the lower rate of interest, and even should they invest the loans under the terms of the loan agreement, they will simply transfer other funds to areas of greater profitability. The end result will be a lack of significant change in the total level of investment in the agricultural sector. This occurs when farmers are rational profit seekers and are in a position to substitute funds between investment possibilities. Larger borrowers are likely to have greater potential for substitution and therefore will be more likely to substitute rural credit for other sources of borrowing. Ultimately, the rural credit programs fail to change the share of investment in agriculture as a share of total investment, unless the return to agriculture changes (Sayad, 1979). Furthermore, the massive flow of credit to a minority of Brazilian farmers is likely, therefore, to further exacerbate problems of income distribution within the agricultural sector, a subject we shall return to later in this study.

Input Subsidies

Fertilizer
        Fertilizers are an important element in Brazilian agriculture. Their use has expanded significantly during the last two decades, amounting to an annual compound growth rate of over 18 percent. By far the most heavily used nutrients are phosphates (46 percent), followed by potassium (32 percent), with nitrogen (22 percent) substantially less (World Bank, 1979a, 55). The high use of phosphates is related to soybean production. Fertilizer usage is heavily skewed towards specific crops (Table 3-11) and between regions (Table 3-12).
        As can be seen, soybeans are the main user of fertilizer, followed by wheat and coffee. The highest use, on a regional basis, is found in the Southeast and Center-West, followed by the South. Total consumption in the North and Northeast only amounts to 10 percent.
        An important target for government policy, often beset with conflicting goals, from 1948 until 1953 fertilizers were included in the "very essential" category, thus freeing importers from the necessity of obtaining import licenses. During the following period, from 1953 to 1957, fertilizers also received preferential treatment as far as imports were concerned. The beginning of protection for the Brazilian domestic fertilizer industry came in 1966 as the production

Table 3-11   Distribution of Fertilizer Consumption
by Crop, 1975-77 (%)

Crop	1975	1976	1977
Cotton	2.5	3.1	3.1
Rice	10.4	8.1	7.7
Potatoes	3.2	3.1	3.0
Coffee	8.3	11.9	11.4
Sugar	16.6	14.8	14.4
Oranges	2.8	2.4	2.3
Corn	9.1	8.1	7.6
Soybeans	21.9	20.8	21.0
Wheat	11.6	11.9	10.4
Other	13.6	15.8	19.1
	100.0	100.0	100.0

Source: World Bank, 1979a.

Table 3-12   Distribution of Fertilizer Consumption
by Region, 1965-78 (%)

Year	North-Northeast	Center	South
1965	7.3	77.9	14.8
1966	10.0	76.9	13.4
1967	9.1	71.9	19.0
1968	6.4	73.1	20.5
1969	8.3	67.7	24.0
1970	8.9	64.8	26.3
1971	8.2	60.0	30.9
1972	8.7	54.3	37.0
1973	8.4	62.5	29.1
1974	9.3	58.2	32.5
1975	6.8	64.7	28.5
1976	10.8	65.0	24.2
1977	9.9	62.5	27.6
1978	9.9	60.6	29.5

Source: World Bank, 1979a.

of fertilizers was seized on by the government as a means of
furthering their ISI aims.   This was reflected in a contin-
gency system for imports, with the right to import duty-free
contingent on distributors acquiring a certain ratio of the
domestic product at a much higher price.   Effectively, farm-

ers were paid a weighted average of fertilizer from the two sources. As a result, the Brazilian domestic fertilizer industry underwent a period of considerable expansion both in volume and in sophistication of end product. By 1980 the domestic share of total consumption had risen to around 45 percent, including 54 percent of phosphate fertilizers and 54 percent of nitrogen; all potassium fertilizers are imported due to a lack of raw materials in Brazil (World Bank, 1979a).

The heavily supported producers in the domestic fertilizer industry kept prices to the farmer well above the world market prices, however despite this the relative price compared to farm product prices improved substantially between the mid 1960s and the late 1970s as international prices of fertilizers fell and world farm product prices improved. This no doubt contributed to the dramatic rise in consumption referred to above. The only years this was not so were those immediately following the oil crisis in 1974, when the situation was abruptly reversed. In 1975 and 1976 the government intervened by providing a 40 percent subsidy on fertilizer purchases. This was yet another example of conflicting objectives as the Brazilian government sought to stimulate both farm consumption and industrial development. The actual level of protection provided to the domestic fertilizer industry varied from year to year, reflecting the volatility of the international fertilizer market. Although fertilizer price differentials of up to 40 percent existed between Brazilian and U.S. farmers, particularly in the case of phosphates which were of major importance to soybean farmers, this was to a large extent compensated by the generous financing for fertilizer purchases through the Banco do Brasil which, until 1978, were offered at zero interest (World Bank, 1979a). Depending on the prevailing rate of inflation, the actual subsidy involved could amount to a substantial part of the total value of the loan. Later loans for fertilizer were subject to the same interest rates as other agricultural production credit, but still at heavily subsidized real interest rates.

Tractors

The Brazilian tractor industry was also subject to ISI policies. Prior to 1960, Brazil had no domestic tractor manufacturing capacity, and all tractors were imported. The multiple exchange rate system was applicable to tractors and imports were therefore encouraged. From the early 1960s, Brazil's domestic tractor industry was heavily supported with substantial tariffs on imported machines. However, liberal credit was again made available for financing tractor purch-

ases. Much foreign capital was invested in Brazilian tractor
and farm machinery plants, encouraged by the high level of
protection which enabled tractors to be manufactured and sold
at prices which would not normally have been competitive in
such a relatively small market (Schuh, 1970).

A related peripheral issue appeared to be that much of
the plant was secondhand, and manufacturers tended toward
supplying machines originally designed for conditions in
developed countries, albeit at a lower level of technology
than was then being supplied in those countries. By the
1970s the tariffs on imported tractors were 30 percent and on
combine harvesters, between 30 and 40 percent.

IMPORT SUBSTITUTION--WHEAT SUPPORT POLICY

Background

The Brazilian government's wheat support policy is
highly significant for three main reasons: first, because it
stands as the only example of an ISI policy which was
directed at agricultural support; second, because wheat and
soybeans are to a large extent complementary crops which are
able to make use of the same capital plant; and third,
because the huge infrastructure, created under the wheat
support scheme, was available to switch directly into soybean
growing when climatic and market conditions proved unsuitable
for the production of wheat (Broadbent and Dixon, 1976). To
this extent it provides an example of a policy specifically
designated for one crop which in fact strongly encouraged
another.

The wheat support scheme was undoubtedly based on the
premise that wheat was the only agricultural commodity being
imported in large quantities, and at the height of the period
of ISI in the 1950s, that wheat was an important part of
Brazilian food consumption. Therefore, any mitigation of
consumer prices would have a beneficial impact on the rate of
inflation. In addition, there appeared by then to be ample
evidence that developing countries could achieve significant
success with wheat production through the transfer of technology already available in the developed countries, or from
the newly emerging research institutions. Wheat policy
objectives were therefore drawn from a multiplicity of
national goals including self sufficiency, the control of
inflation, and lowering food costs to urban consumers. These
were not mutually exclusive goals, however, and it has been

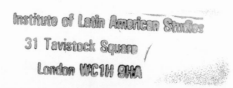

pointed out that the substantial consumer subsidies led to significant increases in demand. This in turn led to higher wheat imports, particularly in years of poor harvest (World Bank, 1979a, 42). The distorted wheat price also had an effect on the demand for competitive crops, with traditional crops such as cassava and maize becoming relatively more expensive than wheat.

It must be borne in mind that wheat support already had a long history in Brazil. There is some evidence of policies intended to stimulate wheat production dating as far back as 1534, the crop having been introduced to Brazil by the early colonists, and in 1749 into Rio Grande do Sul which had long been Brazil's leading wheat area (Knight, 1969, 84). Wheat was regarded by Europeans as an essential staple and higher wheat consumption was regarded as a sign of economic progress. However, growing the crop in Brazil was not without severe problems and expansion of the area planted proceeded only slowly, with insignificant increases in yield (see Table 3-13). Wheat is not ideally suited to Brazil's subtropical southern climate, and the level of technology required for production, in particular for dealing with diseases and pests, is extremely important. Wheat has now become an important crop in Parana, producing more than Rio Grande do Sul, and somewhat more than Sao Paulo. There has also been some development of wheat production on the frontier in Mato Grosso do Sul. Little is grown elsewhere as Table 3-14 shows.

Operation

The principal method of encouraging wheat production in Brazil has been through price support policies. Through the years 1947 to 1952, wheat was supported through the minimum price system. Toward the end of this period, however, the fixed exchange rate, together with falling international prices, led to millers leaning increasingly to favor imports. The Bank of Brazil was made the sole supplier to the mills, which were required to use at least 25 percent domestic wheat in their mix. In 1953 there was an intensification of the wheat expansion program, and a system of multiple exchange rates were established under which wheat could be imported at the lowest rate. A dual price system was introduced which forced millers to pay a higher price for domestic wheat. Quotas were imposed on millers which forbade them to officially, obtain imported wheat until they had used a specific amount of domestic wheat. This led to a substantial amount of fraud (Knight, 1971).

Table 3-13   Brazil: Wheat Production, 1960-82

Year	Area (000 Ha)	Yield (Kg/Ha)	Production (000 MT)	Growth (1960=100)
1960	1,146	622	713	100
1961	1,022	530	545	76
1962	743	950	706	99
1963	793	490	392	55
1964	734	880	643	90
1965	767	760	585	82
1966	717	860	615	86
1967	831	760	629	88
1968	970	880	856	120
1969	1,407	980	1,374	193
1970	1,895	970	1,844	259
1971	2,269	886	2,011	282
1972	2,320	424	983	138
1973	1,839	1,105	2,032	285
1974	2,471	1,157	2,859	401
1975	2,931	610	1,788	251
1976	3,533	906	3,200	449
1977	2,800	738	2,066	290
1978	2,811	957	2,690	377
1979	3,830	764	2,927	411
1980	3,122	865	2,702	379
1981	1,920	1,151	2,209	310
1982	2,825	644	1,820	255

Source: <u>Anuario Estatistico</u>, IBGE,
Rio de Janeiro—various years.

Table 3-14   Brazil: Wheat Production by State, 1960-80
(000 Hectares)

State	1960	1965	1970	1975	1980
Sao Paulo	8	5	19	123	176
Parana	91	91	288	800	1,440
Santa Catarina	116	98	119	68	12
Rio Grande do Sul	1,229	571	1,468	1,899	1,359
Mato Grosso	0	1	1	41	122
Others	2	1	0	0	13
Brazil	1,446	767	1,895	2,931	3,122

Source: <u>Anuario Estatistico</u>, IBGE, Rio de Janeiro—various
years

In 1962, the Bank of Brazil was made sole purchaser for all domestic wheat, the intention being that the bank was to remove price uncertainty by the establishment of fixed or guaranteed prices. The actual prices are announced by the Brazilian Domestic Wheat Purchasing Commission (CTRIN) one year before planting. In 1973-1974, the year of high Soviet grain purchases, the domestic price actually fell below the international price. Subsequently, in 1975, domestic wheat prices were raised to the international level where they have remained ever since. Hence, more or less continuously since 1973, there has been virtually no producer price subsidy (World Bank, 1979a, 90). The government also encouraged the setting up of wheat cooperatives to improve marketing and husbandry practices together with production technology. In addition, wheat has been a considerable beneficiary of subsidized credit. It has been suggested that the stabil- ization of the wheat price did not stabilize producer incomes. In a free market, when harvests are good, the price tends to fall; the reverse occurs when harvests are poor. The movement of price and quantity in different directions tends, over time, to stabilize incomes. Fixing the wheat price obviously precluded this from happening; when harvests were poor, farm income fell, and harvests were indeed frequently poor. (Gulliver, 1981).

Impact on Soybeans

As shown in Table 3-13, the wheat acreage increased from the 1950s until 1962, and then again from 1966 on, when there was a fresh impetus to the program. The soybean-wheat rotation emerged between 1962 and 1968: this was in many ways a logical event. Wheat varieties in use at the time in Brazil were not yet high nitrogen users and nitrogen was an expensive input. Soybeans were available. There had already been some development work at the Sao Paulo research center in Campinas and since soybeans are leguminous—-nitrogen fixing—-they were viewed as a good crop to grow in harness with wheat. Thus farmers could better utilize fixed plant and reduce input costs, in addition the crop slotted in well with the wheat planting and harvesting seasons. The wheat-soybean rotation became accepted both in Parana, in the south where moisture was sufficient, and to a higher degree in Rio Grande do Sul. However, even at the height of its popularity, this rotation was operated only on a small fraction of the total wheat acreage (Gulliver, 1981).
    Later, as technology advanced and higher yields were sought, problems with the rotation began to arise as longer

maturing varieties of soybeans were developed which required earlier planting, preferably in October or November. This meant that wheat would have to have been harvested one or two months before the optimum, or the soybean crop would be planted very late. Hence in recent years, as double cropping incurred a yield penalty, the practice lost much of its attraction. As the significance of soybeans as a commercial crop grew, so did the need to maximize yields. Hence it has been suggested that whereas they were complementary crops at the early part of the cycle, they were later to become substitutes. Both of these phases therefore had considerable significance for the initial expansion of the soybean crop in Brazil.

MARKETING POLICIES

Domestic Consumption Policies

Brazil has maintained a series of policies aimed at adjusting domestic food consumption which has had a direct influence on soybeans. In the 1950s and 1960s the edible oil supply rarely satisfied demand; during that period consumers relied in the main upon cotton seed, peanut oil, and lard. Urbanization and rising per capita income, saw an increase in demand for fats and a concomitant shift in preference from lard to vegetable oils. This put increasing pressure on the price of soybean oil. In an effort to contain price increases and combat inflation, the Brazilian government applied price ceilings on several food items, including soybean oil. This resulted in periodic shortages as either not enough was produced or the crushers built up inventory in an effort to force the government to raise the price ceiling. Shortages eventually became extreme and the price ceiling on soybean oil was abandoned in 1981 (Williams and Thompson, 1984a).

Export Policies

Numerous adjustments in export taxes, subsidies, quotas, and other programs have been made to keep some control over exports of soybeans, soybean oil, and soybean meal. The objectives of these policy initiatives was to ensure adequate supplies of oil and meal to the domestic market, stimulate use of soybean products and expand the domestic crushing capacity (see Chapter 6). The general policy maintained domestic price ceilings on meal and oil, and established export quotas to prevent prices from rising above these ceilings. In addition, bean exports were strictly controlled to ensure positive crushing margins for the crushing industry. In 1982 the quota system was abolished, although export restrictions still could be used at any time to ensure adequate supplies to the rapidly growing domestic oil and meal market (Williams and Thompson, 1984a).

During the 1950s and early 1960s the Brazilian government's highly restrictive attitude to exports, in the wake of ISI policies saw exports of many goods stagnate. Furthermore, the government's anti-export bias was demonstrated in its "exportable surplus" approach to trade (Schuh, 1970). The government first determined whether the domestic market had been adequately supplied before allowing any surplus to be exported. The criterion of domestic price level was used to determine the adequacy of supplies to the home market.

After 1964 and the food supply crisis, the ISI policies were substantially softened and promotion of exports was once more encouraged. In 1967 the system of mini-devaluations was introduced to bring the exchange rate more in line with world currencies. The consequent downward movement in the value of the Cruzeiro stimulated exports, including soybeans. However, exporters were restricted to exporting only three tons of soybeans to one ton of beans or meal equivalent sold on the domestic market, again as an incentive to expand the domestic crushing industry. In addition, a value-added tax was applied to soybean exports at the rate of 12.5 percent, whereas meal exports only attracted a rate of 5 percent and tax on sales of domestic meal was set at zero. This heavy differential provided a major incentive to the domestic crushers and exports of whole soybeans dwindled to virtually nothing. In order to support domestic consumers there was in a virtual embargo on the export of soybean oil prior to 1975.

Throughout the 1970s various controls were introduced, removed, and reintroduced. Particularly at the time of the oil crisis, various parties in the soybean market came under pressure. When world soybean prices rose, the Brazilian feed industry sought relief, and when domestic soybean oil prices increased, the government once more restricted oil exhorts through the foreign trade office of the Banco do Brasil (CACEX) (Williams and Thompson, 1984a).

STRUCTURAL POLICIES

One of the most salient features of Brazilian agriculture is the distribution pattern of agricultural land. A
structural pattern dictated by Brazil's historical colonization and early settlement, the land tenure system has been
faulted for many of Brazil's contemporary development
problems. Successive governments have, over many years, made
tentative efforts to adjust land tenure but with little
evidence of genuine conviction, rather seeking to avoid the
issue through the continuing exploitation of the frontier.

In 1964, the Brazilian Institute of Agrarian Reform
(IBRA) was established under the Brazilian Land Statute of
that year in order to promote land redistribution and land
taxation. It was provided with four instruments: regular-
ization of titles, colonization, expropriation in the
national interest, and a rural land tax. In the area of land
reform virtually nothing was accomplished other than to deal
with land expropriation for such purposes as hydroelectric
projects, highway construction, and urban development. The
land tax, levied annually, was a complex function of farm
size, distance from markets, type of tenure, and potential
productivity, all measured against a specified standard.
There were many exemptions (such as holdings of 25 hectares
or less worked as a family farm) and in any event, the land
tax proved far less progressive than had been intended. The
total tax raised was fairly minimal.

In 1969–1970, in an attempt to pursue its original aims,
the land tax was reformed and IBRA became the National
Institute of Colonization and Agrarian Reform (INCRA) and
adopted new functions. These included the promotion of
"transamazonian colonization," rural electrification, and the
supervision of cooperatives, both rural and urban (Quintana,
1982). The new land tax was aimed at improving utilization
through higher productivity of farm land, as failure to meet
minimum utilization standards increased the tax burden.
However, as with all taxes in Brazil, their effectiveness is
dependent on how rigorously they are enforced. In this case,
INCRA is the enforcement agency.

RESEARCH, EXTENSION, AND EDUCATION

Research and Extension

It is generally accepted that research and extension are of paramount importance in agriculture, particularly in a development situation (see Chapter 2). By and large, the impetus for both is in the hands of government, although in the case of Brazil the initial steps toward setting up a research and extension system emanated from private foundations. Without a generalized, effective research base and an efficient means for disseminating the knowledge gained, there will be a tendency to implement known technology, or technology that is easily transferable from elsewhere regardless of appropriateness. This was the case with soybeans in the early years of the crop's expansion.

Brasil had had for some time a relatively large number of agricultural research institutions covering, a wide geographic area. These varied, however, in the work they were engaged in, both in quality and quantity (Schuh, 1970, 227). During the immediate postwar period, a considerable amount of biological research was undertaken. However, with the onset of the ISI era in the 1950s, agricultural research began to decline. In the 1960s there was fresh recognition of the importance of research, and new funds were injected. Altogether, with the exception of the state of Sao Paulo, it was a low-key operation in the beginning. The matter was complicated by the involvement in agricultural research of both state and federal governments. There was little formal extension, and the extension which was available was separate from the research establishments. Schuh, writing at the latter end of the 1960s, identified several major problems in the research field, although there had been considerable progress in some areas, notably coffee, cotton, and hybrid corn. In 1963-1964, research into soybeans began in earnest in Sao Paulo.

It was not until 1973 that there was a major change in Brazilian government policy in the research field. In that year the Brazilian Agricultural Research Enterprise (EMBRAPA) was created, along with the Brazilian Enterprise for Technical Assistance and Rural Extension (EMBRATER). This heralded the start of a massive program to reorganize investment in agricultural technology. The main objective was to increase yields by providing farmers with both the means and the incentive to absorb new technology (Duran, 1979).

EMBRAPA acts as the central coordinating agency, covering state and federal research institutions, the universities, and private organizations. Most important is

the state of Sao Paulo, long-standing leader in Brazilian
agricultural research. It was estimated in 1978 that public
research expenditures equal about one percent of agricultural
value added, by far the highest proportion of any Latin
American country (World Bank, 1979a, 68). However, from the
data that is available it is clear that the South and
Southeast has been getting the bulk of the research resources, although an effort was made toward the end of the
1970s to redistribute the existing pattern of government
investment in research toward the Northeast.

Education

Outside the direct agricultural policy sphere, but well
within the range of important general policies which affect
agriculture, stands education. Smith, writing in 1967,
suggested that not only is the level of education in agriculture extremely low, but there was no tendency for any real
improvement in rural education. The lack of agricultural
trade schools in particular, in a nation where 50 percent of
the working population was then in still in agriculture,
should have been of particular concern (Smith, 1979). This
view is supported by Schuh, who saw Brazil as not fully
recognizing the contribution that investment in the education
of its people could make in achieving higher rates of
economic growth (Schuh, 1970). Although there have been
substantial improvements in recent years, throughout this
period the low level of general education in rural areas, and
the lack of specialist agricultural trade schools in particular, together with the very limited access to advanced
higher education, was to act as a substantial brake on rural
areas and their development.

4
The Development
of the Brazilian
Soybean Industry

INTRODUCTION

In the 1970s Brazil became one of the leading producers, first of whole soybeans and later of soybean products, in the world, and the second largest exporter after the United States. To grow from a negligible tonnage before 1960 to an annual output in excess of 15 million metric tons by 1980 was a substantial achievement by any standards (see Table 4-1). However, the development of the soybean industry has to be put into context with Brazilian agriculture as a whole, its stage of development, the policies impacting on it, and the resources which were available or became available as the soybean expansion began to gather momentum from the early 1960s until the end of the following decade.

EARLY YEARS

Much of the literature on soybeans in Brazil, attribute their introduction to Japanese immigrant farmers who introduced the crop in the 1920s. In fact, soybeans are mentioned in Brazil's Jornal do Agricultor in the issue of September 10, 1882, referring to the botanical characteristics of the plant and alluding to experiments in the state of Bahia. As a commercial crop it remained of little significance until after World War II. At first the crop was confined almost exclusively to the southernmost state of Rio Grande do Sul, and the area planted was modest.

Table 4-1   Soybean: Area, Yield, Production, and Growth:
Brazil, 1960-82

Year	Area (000 Ha)	Yield (Kg/Ha)	Production (000 MT)	Growth (1960=100)
1960	171	1200	206	100
1961	241	1127	271	132
1962	314	1005	345	167
1963	340	950	323	157
1964	360	848	305	148
1965	432	1212	523	254
1966	491	1213	595	289
1967	612	1169	716	348
1968	850	906	654	317
1969	906	1166	1057	513
1970	1319	1190	1509	733
1971	1589	1250	1977	960
1972	2274	1250	3666	1780
1973	3616	1386	5009	2432
1974	5143	1531	9876	4794
1975	5824	1698	9893	4802
1976	6417	1749	11227	5450
1977	7070	1770	12513	6074
1978	7778	1226	9535	4629
1979	7321	1360	9959	4834
1980	8774	1727	15156	7357
1981	8485	1765	14978	7271
1982	8202	1562	12810	6218

Source: Anuario Estatistico, IBGE, Rio do
Janeiro—various years.

Even as late as the mid-1950s, less than 75,000 hectares of
soybeans were planted, yielding as little as 100,000 tons.
By the early 1960s the Brazilian area planted in
soybeans had virtually quintupled. At this time, still more
than 90 percent was being grown in Rio Grande do Sul (see
Table 4-2). Small quantities were being grown in other
states but the areas involved and quantities produced remained negligible until well into the 1960s. To a limited
degree, research had been taking place for a number of years,
and contacts were maintained between Brazilian researchers
and their counterparts in the United States; indeed virtually
all the varieties then grown originated in North America,
although cooperation on a national basis appears to have been

limited to meetings of a few groups of researchers (Hymowitz, 1968).

Table 4-2   Soybean Area Planted:
             Rio Grande do Sul and Brazil, 1952-62

Year	Rio Grand do Sul Area (000 Ha)	Brazil Area (000 Ha)	RGS/Brazil %
1952	58.8	60.0	98.0
1953	61.4	63.0	97.5
1954	62.1	68.0	91.3
1955	67.3	74.0	90.9
1956	73.0	81.0	90.1
1957	78.2	97.0	80.6
1958	92.9	107.0	86.8
1959	104.0	114.0	91.2
1960	159.4	171.0	93.2
1961	227.0	241.0	94.2
1962	295.0	314.0	93.9

Source: Calculated from Anuario Estatistico
        --various years

Nevertheless, there was strong interest in developing the soybean crop in Brazil, in particular in the center and south of the country. The first important research center was in Campinas, in the state of Sao Paulo, although the crop was never to achieve the same predominance in that state it did in Rio Grande do Sul or Parana. The primary appeal at first was to be closely associated with wheat. As discussed earlier, the wheat and soybean crops were very much intertwined in Rio Grande do Sul, particularly during the early days of soybean development. There are a variety of other reasons why Rio Grande do Sul became the springboard for the explosion of the soybean which, after establishing itself firmly there, went on to become a major crop in several other states.

     Ideal growing conditions prevail in much of Rio Grande do Sul; the land tenure structure, the fertile soils and ample moisture and the large farms with their well-established farmers, began early on to demonstrate some of the potential in the soybean crop. However, it was its use as a complementary crop to wheat (as a double crop, taking advantage of the substantial infrastructure that had already been created under the Government's ISI-based wheat support policies) that caused soybeans to take off as a commercial crop in the 1950s. As has been mentioned, wheat remained a crop of many problems. A high incidence of pest and fungal attacks made the crop very hard to manage. The low-yielding wheat varieties suitable for Brazilian conditions were not responsive to the high levels of nitrogen usage associated with the wheat crops of the Green Revolution elsewhere, the Brazilian subtropical climate was not ideal for what is mainly a temperate crop, and the net result was disappointing yields and variable returns. However, the considerable production infrastructure already created under the wheat support policies was ideal for utilization with a second crop. Soybeans could be grown in the inter-season, utilizing some of the surplus nutrients from the wheat crop and providing sufficient nitrogen for the requirements of the relatively low demands of Brazilian wheat which would follow. The ability to spread the amortization of fixed plant over two crops greatly reduced the unit fixed costs of growing both wheat and soybeans.

It was estimated that by the early 1960s about 20 percent of the soybean acreage was already fully mechanized (Hymowitz, 1968), comparable to mechanization in the United States. This demonstrated the ease of transfer of an existing technology to a country which was, certainly in agriculture, at a far less advanced stage of development, yet where growing conditions were similar. Mechanized farming was largely confined to the southern part of Rio Grande do Sul and the high plateau where the farms were large; farmers either rented or owned 200 to 1000 hectares of flat, easy working land. In the north of the state very different conditions prevailed. First, the land was undulating, and second, it was farmed as holdings of 10 to 15 hectares, largely by German and Italian immigrants, who had a background of mixed farming. However, after the initial introduction of soybeans on the larger farms, the crop was soon to become popular on much smaller farms. Originally plantings were mixed, but some adopted a more or less monoculture system before long. It was on these farms that much of the planting was soon to be found. Sowing and harvesting of the crop in this area was almost entirely dependent on hand labor. Most of the early soybean planting was as interrow cropping, one or two rows of soybeans between two rows of corn. As farmers grew in experience, they gradually moved toward more specialized cropping.

The situation in the remaining states was similarly divided according to the pattern of land ownership and traditional cropping. In Parana and Santa Catarina, where the great majority of growers were small farmers, the methods of production were similar to northern Rio Grande do Sul, with soybeans often intercropped with coffee, corn, or cassava; however, in Sao Paulo where the farms were larger, the area of soybeans remained quite small but the development of agriculture was far superior to any other region in the country, and the operation was highly mechanized.

There is no doubt that during by 1950s soybeans had already become an established crop in Brazil, achieving a planted area of 114,000 hectares by 1959, having grown from virtually nothing (18,000 tons) in 1948. However, even the virtual tripling of the area within the next three years left it a crop of little significance to Brazilian agriculture, or the Brazilian economy as a whole, and gave no portent of the massive expansion soybean production was to experience over the next two decades.

MAJOR EXPANSION: 1964-1982

By 1963 the Brazilian soybean industry was firmly established. Over the next two decades output was to grow by a factor of 46, and to become a significant part of both the agricultural and the national economy. Within a dozen years it was to rival coffee as a major export and foreign exchange earner, making it a very substantial contributor to Brazil's balance of trade.

Within the geographic area of Brazil, soybeans are produced in 8 of the 25 states to some degree; but in only 5 states is the crop of any real significance: Rio Grande do Sul, Parana, Santa Catarina, Sao Paulo and Mato Grosso (Mato Gross was subdivided into Mato Grosso and Mato Grosso do Sul in the late 1970s with virtually all the soybean cultivation being found largely in Mato Gross do Sul. For our purposes these two states will still be regarded as one). The breakdown in terms of quantities produced per state, and the relative importance of each state within Brazil's soybean production as a whole are shown in Table 4-3 and Figure 4-1. The soybean areas are different from their counterparts in North America, being sub-tropical in climate virtually throughout. Cultivation of soybeans is very similar in many respects to the Midwest of the United States, particularly in the west of the region, although the soils are inherently less fertile and the weather far more variable. In the south of the region there is more moisture and a more humid environment. Here the crop is grown in part on more un-

dulating land, and the countryside is closer in type to
Georgia or Louisiana than the prairie states. Brazilian soils
are, on the whole, far less fertile than in the United States

Table 4-3   Brazilian Production of Soybeans by State, 1960-82
                              (000 Metric Tons)

State	1960	1962	1965	1967	1970	1974	1976	1978	1980	1982
Rio Grande										
do Sul	188.5	320.8	463.2	550.8	976.8	3870.0	5107.0	4567.8	5737.2	4220.6
Parana	7.4	13.9	44.1	113.3	368.0	2588.9	4500.0	3150.1	5400.2	4200.1
Santa Catarina	3.8	4.1	5.1	9.2	53.0	431.5	409.9	354.7	425.1	534.7
Sao Paulo	3.1	4.6	8.7	38.2	90.1	522.0	765.0	745.5	1099.1	993.3
Mato Grosso	0.4	0.9	0.8	2.7	9.0	307.0	290.4	479.1	1439.3	1902.8
Others	2.5	0.9	1.3	1.4	11.6	156.8	154.2	243.4	1054.9	984.5
BRAZIL	205.7	345.2	523.2	715.6	1508.5	7876.2	11226.5	9540.6	15155.8	12836.0

Percent of Total Production

State	1960	1962	1965	1967	1970	1974	1976	1978	1980	1982
Rio Grande										
do Sul	91.6	92.9	88.5	77.0	64.8	49.1	45.5	47.9	37.9	32.9
Parana	3.6	4.0	8.4	15.8	24.4	32.9	40.1	33.0	35.6	32.7
Santa Catarina	1.8	1.2	1.0	1.3	3.5	5.5	3.7	3.7	2.8	4.2
Sao Paulo	1.5	1.3	1.7	5.3	6.0	6.6	6.8	7.8	7.3	7.7
Mato Grosso	0.2	0.3	0.2	0.4	0.6	3.9	2.6	5.0	9.5	14.8
Others	1.2	0.3	0.2	0.2	0.8	2.0	1.4	2.6	7.0	7.7
BRAZIL	100.0	100.0	100.0	100.0	100.0	100.0	100.0	100.0	100.0	100.0

Source: Calculated from Anuario Estatistico, IBGE, Rio de Janeiro--various years.

It has been estimated that only about 10 percent of the soils
within the total extent of Brazil are without some form of
serious deficiency; these are confined to the interior of Sao
Paulo, north and northwestern Parana, the southern tip of Rio
Grande do Sul, and the undulating uplands to the north of
that state. As one might expect, these areas now tend to be
closely associated with the cultivation of soybeans.
    Tables 4-4 and 4-5 demonstrate the change in importance
of the crop to the soybean producing states. Whereas at the
beginning of the period nearly 92 percent of production came
from Rio Grande do Sul, by 1980 Parana had almost caught up.
Between the two, these states, produced virtually three
quarters of Brazil's output in more or less equal propor-

tions.   A further   ten percent   was produced in Mato Grosso,
leaving the remaining 10 percent divided among other states.

Figure 4-1

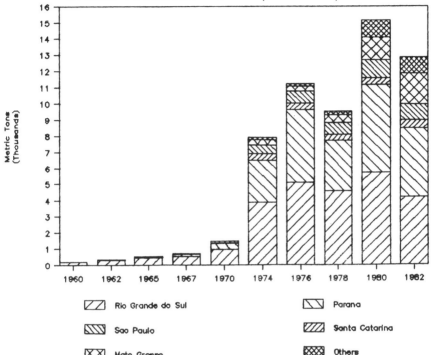

Brazil: Production of Soybeans by State

From the beginning, Rio Grande do Sul has been the
leading soybean producer.   The geographic location of the
state has been of paramount importance to its agricultural
development.   The furthest south of the Brazilian states, it
occupies some 3 percent of Brazil's total land area.   It is
composed of four quite distinct regions: an area between the
Atlantic and the coastal mountain range forming the coastal
plain, the mountainous region itself, a high plateau to the
north and west of the mountains, and finally the low level
plain to the south, covering the largest part of the state.
Each of these areas has a distinct soil type and topography
which, in turn, has dictated the pattern of agriculture in
each region.   The coastal plain with its wet, sandy soils has
the least agricultural significance, although it is now, with
drainage and irrigation, a mixed farming area.   The undulating uplands of the north of the state contain an area of
small mixed farms (the nearest thing to family farms) with

their population of European immigrant farmers and their descendants.

Table 4-4   The Contribution of Soybeans to the Agricultural Economy of Rio Grande do Sul

Year	Area Cultivated (000 Ha)			Value of Production (current Cr$ 000)		
	All Crops	Soybeans	%	All Crops	Soybeans	%
1952-54	2,497.4	60.8	2.43	9,360	181	1.93
1962-64	3,379.6	315.9	9.35	225,510	11,200	4.97
1967-69	4,363.8	565.7	12.96	1,442,520	118,100	8.19
1973-75	6,981.9	2,700.3	38.68	10,923,789	4,584,847	41.97
1980	6,682.6	3,987.5	59.67	132,022,000	53,528,000	40.54

Source: Bowman, 1983

Table 4-5   The Contribution of Soybeans to the Agricultural Economy of Parana

Year	Area Cultivated (000 Ha)			Value of Production (current Cr$ 000)		
	All Crops	Soybeans	%	All Crops	Soybeans	%
1960	3197.04	5.06	0.16	66,209	54	0.08
1970	5653.49	368.01	6.51	2,305,871	105,508	4.58
1974	7060.69	1340.00	18.98	12,255,103	2,466,343	20.13
1980	7097.79	2410.80	33.97	132,466,000	44,905,000	33.90

Source: Bowman, 1983.

The open plain of the high plateau was traditionally cattle-grazing country and was the first area of the interior of the state to be settled, having been divided into large estates for cattle rearing and beef production. On the larger farms livestock still predominates. It was, however, in the southern part of this region that there was a substantial move into mechanized wheat production in response to the economic incentives of the late 1950s and early 1960s, later to be followed by soybeans. It was this area that became Brazil's first soybean "frontier" in the mid-1960s.

The low-lying plains of the south of the state consist of an area of high-quality, natural grassland known as

"Gaucho Country" and is, as the name suggests, a continuation of the pampas and open grazing lands of Uruguay and the Argentine to the south. It is an area, for the most part, of very large farms, concentrating upon cattle and sheep which are grazed extensively, with some smaller mixed farms interspersed throughout the area. Following the incentives to expand wheat production and the onset of the soybean boom, there has been a continuing trend toward ploughing up the traditional grasslands although cropping remains at less than 15 percent of the total area. Much of the cropping that developed has been carried on by "renters," usually from the north of the state, who rent the land from the large estates and cultivate it for a few years before returning it to grazing.

It was, therefore, the expansion of the wheat crop in Rio Grande do Sul which provided the spring-board for soybeans. The close relationship between the two crops is significant. In the early days they developed simultaneously; later, however, soybeans expanded at a much faster rate than wheat. This was largely because the relationship between wheat and soybeans changed from one of being complementary to being substitutes. In addition, as soybeans became more attractive as a crop in their own right, through economic factors and government support, the expansion gathered pace. As Table 4-5 demonstrates, the soybean area, in Rio Grande do Sul, expanded from 2 percent in value of all crops in 1952-1954, to 42 percent by 1973-1975. This illustrates the enormous importance soybeans have attained as a crop in the state. The details of land use, cropping substitution, and cropping patterns will be discussed in Chapter 5.

Parana is Brazil's second largest soybean producer and, by 1980 had almost drawn level with Rio Grande do Sul. Situated immediately to the north of Santa Catarina, Rio Grande do Sul's northern neighbor, Parana is the northernmost state in Brazil's southern region, and is slightly smaller and very different geographically from Rio Grande do Sul. Much of the state is covered by natural forest, and the forestry industry is a significant part of Parana's rural economy. Traditional mixed crops are produced, particularly in the north. Arable cropping, in general, has shown considerable expansion in recent years.

Much of the rapid expansion of the soybean crop in Parana during the 1960s came as a result of the Brazilian coffee eradication scheme. Northern Parana is the only part of the southern region which can produce coffee, and in spite of severe climatic difficulties, particularly very severe frosts, coffee production has been highly successful. Some soybeans, as well as other crops, were inter-planted between the rows of coffee, but it was the Brazilian coffee erad-ication scheme which resulted in much of Parana's soybean growth in the 1960s. Because of a world glut in coffee and the consequent low market prices, farmers were encouraged through payment to eradicate their coffee plants and were given a free choice on substitute cropping. Many chose soybeans. In addition, wheat production began to build up in the state during the 1960s and soybean was double-cropped with wheat. In the 1970s, with various economic incentives including substantially higher prices for soybeans, the crop began to expand on its own merits across Parana's fertile soils, particularly to the west of the state. Table 4-4 shows the growing importance of the soybean crop to Parana over this period.

Sao Paulo and Santa Catarina also produce soybeans but neither has produced even as much as 8 percent of Brazil's total output. They do not have the same significance in the production pattern as the two states previously described. Sao Paulo however, was generally regarded as Brazil's most industrialized and agriculturally developed state. It produced 50 percent and 30 percent of Brazil's national output respectively, and occupied third position in produc-tion of Brazil's soybean states throughout the 1970s. The state has some of Brazil's most fertile soils. Its early agricultural development, its urbanization, and its well developed markets for agricultural produce worked together to create a diverse and efficient agriculture. Most of Brazil's coffee is produced in Sao Paulo, as are most of Brazil's other major crops. Soybeans were slow to gain popularity, and they have remained a fairly insignificant crop in the state. The profitability level of other crops and the lack of any specific reason to change to soybeans kept the relative contribution of the crop at a low level. Although there was a considerable expansion of soybeans in the 1970s, and although by 1982 Sao Paulo was producing as many soybeans as Rio Grande do Sul had at the beginning of the decade, in terms of contribution to Brazil's total soybean area or the state's total agricultural area, the soybean crop remained insignificant.

Santa Catarina is of far less agricultural significance than either of the three states mentioned above. Situated immediately to the south of Parana, and due north of Rio Grand do Sul, the high plateau grasslands of the latter extend into the state. Such areas of soybeans as do exist here are found on these. Because of the undulating terrain, Santa Catarina is generally unsuitable for commercial arable cultivation. Dairying and rice production are found to the north of the state, and cattle predominate in the central areas. Soybean production, although expanding rapidly between 1970 and the end of the decade, showed no sign of the massive growth found in the two neighboring states. Yields also have been disappointing, suggesting that soybeans were being grown on more marginal land.

Mato Grosso is the final significant region for soybeans. Forming Brazil's Center-West region together with the state of Goias, they represent virtually a quarter of the nation's land area. The southern part of Mato Grosso, which became Mato Grosso do Sul in the late 1970s, and the southernmost part of Goias, are currently the only areas of agricultural importance. This region is still very much regarded as the agricultural frontier in Brazil, and has more recently become an important soybean producing area with substantial potential for further development. Most of the region is utilized for extensive cattle grazing, and virtually all the arable cropping, including soybean development, has been confined to the south. The state's characteristic open, flat lands have deep soils, and are relatively fertile and easy to cultivate. They have proved a faster and simpler means of expanding national soybean output than intensification of the more traditional areas, either through redistribution of land or through technological progress. The state is situated due west of Sao Paulo, on the Paraguay border, and its favorable climate and topography together with its access to Sao Paulo makes it attractive for further agricultural expansion.

Development of the soybean crop started there in earnest in the early 1970s and since then, expansion has been rapid. The provision of substantial quantity of investment and production credit at low rates of interest made soybeans an attractive proposition. Several cooperatives from the Rio Grande do Sul moved into the area to service farmers who had moved north. From modest beginnings early in the decade, production had risen above 300,000 tons by 1975, and within five years this was to quintuple to exceed 1.5 million tons. The remaining sectors of the Center-West are, as yet, insignificant in terms of soybean production. The shorter growing season to the north makes cultivation with existing varieties impractical, and without major agronomic developments this area is likely to remain marginal in the foreseeable future.

As for the remaining areas of Brazil, Goias produces around 500,000 tons per annum, and the state of Minas Gerais in the Southeast produces a further 300,000. Further expansion is likely to remain in frontier regions or through

technological improvement in the earlier developed areas in
the South.   The land and climate to the North is not regarded
as suitable for the production of soybeans with the prevailing level of technology.

5
Micro Impact—
Primary Production

FARMLAND DEVELOPMENT

FARMLAND DEVELOPMENT

Land Use

Brazil has a vast land area and has remained one of the last of the great "frontier" countries. This section examines the impact of the soybean expansion on land use in Brazil; that is, whether the soybean crop replaced other crops, increased utilization of land within the existing farm areas, or was a factor in extending the frontier still further.

The area of land in Brazil regarded within the census as being farmed, grew from 249.86 to 364.84 million hectares during the period 1960 to 1980. This increase of 46 percent represented an annual growth rate of around 2 percent. The growth in land use for arable crops is shown in Table 5-1.

The most significant crops produced in Brazil are shown in Table 5-2, together with the areas planted and annual yields. The changes over time, demonstrated in index form, are shown in Table 5-3. With the exception of coffee, which suffered a substantial decrease in area planted, and sugar cane, where growth was insignificant, there was an increase in all major crops. These together represented close to 94 percent of arable planting in 1980. The area devoted to corn, amounting to 12.6 million acres, represents the highest single crop. By the 1980s soybeans were a not too distant second, having undergone massive expansion. By 1980, Brazil's soybean area had grown to nearly 18 percent of all arable crop land.

Table 5-1   Brazil: Growth of Arable Crop Area, 1960-80

Region	1960	1970	1980	Proportion of Total (%)	Growth 1960-80	Change 1960-80(%)
North	432,602	613,007	1,743,645	3.55	1,311,043	303.06
Northeast	8,727,700	10,330,493	14,191,950	28.90	5,464,250	62.61
Southeast	9,412,241	9,658,588	12,117,074	24.68	2,704,833	28.74
South	8,144,087	11,076,456	14,571,446	29.67	6,427,359	78.92
Center-West	1,365,879	2,402,899	6,480,145	13.20	5,114,266	374.43
Brazil	28,082,509	34,081,443	49,104,260	100.00	21,021,751	74.86

Source: Censo Agropecuario--IBGE, Rio de Janeiro (various years);
        Anuario Estatistico--IBGE, Rio de Janeiro (various years).

Table 5-2   Area, Production and Yield of Brazil's Main Crops,
                          1962 and 1982

Crop	Production (MT) 1962	Production (MT) 1982	Area (Ha) 1962	Area (Ha) 1982	Yield (MT/Ha) 1962	Yield (MT/Ha) 1982
Corn	7,342,795	21,842,477	9,580,385	12,619,531	0.766	1.731
Soybeans	345,175	12,836,047	313,640	8,203,277	1.101	1.565
Rice	5,556,834	9,734,553	3,349,810	6,024,657	1.659	1.616
Beans	1,708,983	2,902,657	2,716,257	5,926,143	0.629	0.490
Cotton	1,919,605	1,927,977	3,457,857	3,624,217	0.555	0.532
Sugar	62,534,516	186,646,607	1,466,619	3,084,297	42.639	60.515
Wheat	680,465	1,826,945	743,458	2,827,929	0.915	0.646
Cassava	19,843,422	2,407,232	1,476,774	2,122,029	13.437	1.134
Coffee	4,380,607	1,915,861	4,462,657	1,895,486	0.982	1.011
Oranges	6,013,319	57,991,021	125,821	589,967	47.793	98.295
Cacao	464,762	351,149	140,363	533,273	3.311	0.658
Tobacco	47,477	420,329	40,688	317,231	1.167	1.325

Source: Calculated from Anuario Estatistico--IRBG, Brazil.

Table 5-3   Changes in Production, Area, and Yield, 1962-82
(1962 = 100)

Crop	Production (000 MT)		Area (000 Ha)		Yield (MT/Ha)	
	1962	1982	1962	1982	1962	1982
Corn	100	297	100	132	100	226
Soybeans	100	3719	100	2616	100	142
Rice	100	175	100	180	100	97
Beans	100	170	100	218	100	78
Cotton	100	100	100	105	100	96
Sugar	100	298	100	210	100	142
Wheat	100	109	100	380	100	71
Cassava	100	12	100	144	100	8
Coffee	100	43	100	43	100	103
Oranges	100	964	100	469	100	206
Cacao	100	76	100	380	100	20
Tobacco	100	885	100	780	100	114

Source: Calculated from Anuario Estatistico--IRBG--Brazil.

Table 5-4 demonstrates where this growth of almost 8 million hectares occurred. Of the total, 69 percent was confined to just two states in the southern region of the country, Rio Grande do Sul and Parana, and a further 13 percent occurred in the Center-West frontier state of Mato Grosso.

As can be seen from Table 5-1, there was substantial growth in all arable land in Brazil over the two decades in question. In all, the cropping area increased by more than 21 million hectares, in excess of 75 percent. Of this, 42 percent can be attributed to the growth in the soybean area. As one might have expected, the relative growth of arable land was highest in the frontier areas of the Center-West region; however, the highest absolute growth in cropping was in the traditional farming areas in the south of the country. It was in this region that the majority of the soybean expansion took place in the second decade of the period, as shown in Table 5-4.

Hence, the soybean crop appears to have been responsible in large part for the high rate of growth in arable cropping. In addition the location of most of this growth took place in the more developed areas of the south. Therefore, although the development of the frontier was important, it did not play as significant a part as many would believe.

Table 5-4   Brazilian Production of Soybeans 1962 – 82
                   Area Planted by State   (000 Hectares)

State	1962	1965	1967	1974	1976	1978	1980	1982
Rio Grande								
do Sul	294.9	416.3	490.9	2770.0	3296.0	3754.0	3987.5	3539.5
Parana	10.5	54.3	82.9	1340.0	2083.3	2348.5	2410.8	2100.0
Mato Grosso	1.0	1.5	2.3	174.9	191.1	499.6	877.0	1036.9
Santa Caterina	2.6	5.7	7.3	365.0	339.4	408.8	520.4	445.7
Sao Paulo	4.0	12.3	27.7	335.0	394.0	558.8	560.8	516.0
Others	0.6	0.6	1.0	158.3	112.6	212.5	418.4	565.2
BRAZIL	313.6	490.7	612.1	5143.1	6416.4	7782.2	8774.8	8203.3

Percent of Total Brazilian Plantings

State	1962	1965	1967	1974	1976	1978	1980	1982
Rio Grande								
do Sul	94.02	84.84	80.19	53.86	51.37	48.24	45.44	43.15
Parana ·	3.36	11.07	13.55	26.05	32.47	30.18	27.47	25.60
Mato Grosso	0.33	0.30	0.38	3.40	2.98	6.42	9.99	12.64
Santa Caterina	0.82	1.16	1.20	7.10	5.29	5.25	5.93	5.43
Sao Paulo	1.29	2.51	4.52	6.51	6.14	7.18	6.39	6.29
Others	0.19	0.13	0.16	3.08	1.76	2.73	4.77	6.89
BRAZIL	100.0	100.0	100.0	100.0	100.0	100.0	100.0	100.0

Source: Calculated from Anuario Estatistico--IBGE, Rio de Janeiro.

Distribution of Land

     The agrarian structure in Brazil has, justifiably, often
been held responsible for the poor overall performance of
Brazil's Agriculture (Chacel, 1968). The historical settlement of the country was completely different from the
settlement of North America. As outlined in the intro-

duction, Brazil's earliest agricultural development was as a plantation economy which left a legacy in the North and Northeast of the country consisting of a pattern of "latifundio" (enormous estates) and "minifundio" (peasant plots on the periphery). These, together with the tradition of large landowners living in the cities, away from their lands, created a farm structure not conducive to agricultural modernization or social equality. With the decline of the plantations, farming in northern Brazil has remained very much a subsistence agricultural economy, heavily dependent on domestic staple crops such as corn, cassava, and beans.

Table 5-5   Brazil Farm Structure: Distribution of Farms, 1970 and 1980

Farm Size(Ha)	1970 Number	%	Area	%	1980 Number	%	Area	%
Less than 10	2,519,630	51.4	9,083,495	3.1	2,598,019	50.4	9,004,259	2.5
10 to 100	1,934,392	39.4	60,069,704	20.4	2,016,774	39.2	64,494,343	17.7
100 to 1000	414,746	8.5	108,742,676	37.0	488,521	9.5	126,799,188	34.8
1000 to 10000	35,425	0.7	80,059,162	27.2	45,496	0.9	104,548,849	28.7
More than 10000	1,449	0.0	36,190,429	12.3	2,345	0.0	60,007,780	16.4
Total	4,905,642	100	294,145,466	100	5,151,155	100	364,854,419	100

Source: Censo Agropecurario--1980--IBGE, Rio de Janeiro, 1984.

The overall farm structure of Brazil is demonstrated in Table 5-5. The data shows that the number of small farms grew during the period by around 3 percent, and the average size of holdings in the less-than-10 hectare group fell. The situation in main soybean areas in the center and south of the country is less dramatic but still heavily skewed. Tables 5-6 and 5-7 show the details of the land distribution in the two main soybean-growing states as well as the distribution of soybean plantings according to farm in the years 1970 and 1980. As can be seen from Table 5-6, in the case of Rio Grande do Sul the number of small farmers (less

Table 5-6   Rio Grande do Sul: Farm Structure and Soybean Plantings

1970

		Establishments					Soybean Growers					
Farm Size (Ha)	Number	% of Total	Group Area	% of Total Group	Mean	Number	% of Total Group	Area of Soybeans	% of Total Area	% of Soybean Plantings		% of Farm in Soybeans
	A	B	C	D	E = C/A	F	G	H	I	J	K=E*F	L=H/K*100
Less than 10	177,519	34.7	853,462	3.6	4.81	72,577	40.9	150,998	17.69	11.7	348930	43.3
10 to 100	301,069	58.8	7,699,620	32.3	25.57	139,425	46.3	747,262	9.71	57.7	3565693	21.0
100 to 1000	29,827	5.8	8,371,286	35.2	280.66	4,225	14.2	341,635	4.08	26.4	1185794	28.8
1000 to 10000	3,216	0.6	6,530,864	27.4	2030.74	273	8.5	54,764	0.84	4.2	554392	9.9
More than 10000	19	0.0	351,947	1.5	18523.53	3	15.8	491	0.14	0.0	55571	0.9
Totals	511,650	100.0	23,807,179	100.0	46.53	216,503		1,295,150		100.0	10073929	12.9

1980

		Establishments					Soybean Growers					
Farm Size (Ha)	Number	% of Total	Group Area	% of Total Group	Mean	Number	% of Total Group	Area of Soybeans	% of Total Area	% of Soybean Plantings		% of Farm in Soybeans
	A	B	C	D	E = C/A	F	G	H	I	J	K=E*F	L=H/K*100
Less than 10	161,141	33.9	790,087	3.3	4.90	75,922	47.1	218,157	27.61	5.8	372252	58.6
10 to 100	278,362	58.6	7,300,045	30.3	26.23	163,072	58.6	1,779,012	24.37	47.3	4276564	41.6
100 to 1000	31,768	6.7	9,018,708	37.5	283.89	10,538	33.2	1,437,509	15.94	38.3	2991663	48.1
1000 to 10000	3,373	0.7	6,602,953	27.4	1957.59	811	24.0	322,971	4.89	8.6	1587606	20.3
More than 10000	16	0.0	345,817	1.4	21613.56	2	12.5	260	0.08	0.0	43227	0.6
Totals	474,660	100.0	24,057,610	100.0	50.68	250,345		3,757,909		100.0	12688456	29.6

Source: Censo Agropecuario, 1970 & 1980, IBGE--Rio De Janiero

Table 5-7

Parana: Farm Structure and Soybean Plantings

1970

Farm Size (Ha)	Establishments					Soybean Growers						
	Number	% of Total	Group Area	% of Total Group	Mean	Number	% of Total Group	Area of Soybeans	% of Total Area	% of Soybeans Plantings		% of Farm in Soybeans
	A	B	C	D	E=C/A	F	G	H	I	J	K=E*F	L=H/K*100
Less than 10	295,272	53.25	1,575,024	10.77	5.33	53,575	18.14	114,664	7.28	28.98	285777	40.12
10 to 100	240,936	43.45	6,097,366	41.69	25.31	56,818	23.58	224,773	3.69	56.81	1437893	15.63
100 to 1000	17,158	3.09	4,220,749	28.86	245.99	1,558	9.08	49,905	1.18	12.61	383257	13.02
1000 to 10000	1,074	0.19	2,294,765	15.69	2136.65	71	6.61	6,144	0.27	1.55	151702	4.05
More than 10000	13	0.00	437,625	2.99	33663.46	2	15.38	146	0.03	0.04	67327	0.22
Totals	554,453	100	14,625,529	100	26.38	112,024	20.20	395,632	2.71	100.00	2325956	17.01

1980

Farm Size (Ha)	Establishments					Soybean Growers						
	Number	% of Total	Group Area	% of Total Group	Mean	Number	% of Total Group	Area of Soybeans	% of Total Area	% of Soybeans Plantings		% of Farm in Soybeans
	A	B	C	D	E=C/A	F	G	H	I	J	K=E*F	L=H/K*100
Less than 10	214,995	47.36	1,019,970	8.05	4.74	28,894	13.44	90,585	8.88	4.36	137078	66.08
10 to 100	215,031	47.37	5,355,303	42.28	24.90	62,299	28.97	991,096	18.51	47.75	1551544	63.88
100 to 1000	22,349	4.92	4,537,024	35.82	203.01	6,433	28.78	815,476	17.97	39.29	1305950	62.44
1000 to 10000	1,510	0.33	1,677,232	13.24	1110.75	334	22.12	170,463	10.16	8.21	370990	45.95
More than 10000	27	0.01	76,008	0.60	2815.11	5	18.52	8,064	10.61	0.39	14076	57.29
Totals	453,912	100	12,665,537	100	27.90	97,965	21.58	2,075,684	16.39	100.00	3379637	61.42

Source: Censo Agro Pecuario, 1970 & 1980--IBGE, Rio de Janeiro.

77

than 10 hectares) fell substantially over the period, as did the numbers of farms in the 10-to-100 hectare group. At the beginning of soybean expansion in Rio Grande do Sul, nearly 12 percent of the holdings of less than 10 hectares were planting soybeans; however, as the expansion gathered momentum, the proportions changed, with larger farmers, particularly in the 100-to-1000 hectare size group, providing most of the growth.

A similar if not more dramatic change took place in the second largest soybean state, Parana, Table 5-7. During the rapid expansion which took place between 1970 and 1980 (when the acreage of soybeans in the state grew from just under 400,000 hectares to over 2 million), the plantings by the smaller farms showed an actual decline in absolute area as well as in relative proportion, with the massive increase taking place entirely on the larger farms, and much on the very large farms.

The changes in farm size become even more significant when crop type is related to the economic status of the farmer involved. The classification of farms into four levels of tenure: proprietor, renter, share cropper, and squatter, is indicative of what took place. Looking at the situation in Parana between 1970 and 1975, figures show that there was a substantial increase in numbers in the renter and proprietor groups, the share croppers remained unchanged, and the squatter group declined. Of the farms that produced soybeans, expansion was slanted heavily toward the proprietor class, which grew by more than 64 percent (Bowman, 1983). From the analysis above it appears that in terms of land distribution, the main beneficiaries were the wealthier land owners on the larger farms.

Cropping Patterns

One of the most evident and serious consequences of the Brazilian soybean expansion has been the change in cropping patterns, and in particular in the production of domestic staple crops. Table 5-8 shows the significant individual crop plantings for the years 1960, 1970, and 1980, and their percentage contributions to the total arable land under cultivation. Prior to the main soybean expansion during the 1960-1970 period, there were small proportional increases in the contribution of all four major staples: corn, rice, beans, and cassava. When the soybean area began to expand in the subsequent decade, there were absolute increases in the area planted in all four staples, the relative contributions of three of these crops, rice, beans and cassava, fell, while the proportion of corn remained virtually static.

Table 5-8   Brazil: Significant Crops, 1960-80
                   Area (Hectares)

Crop[1]	1960	% of Arable	1970	% of Arable	1980	% of Arable
1. Corn	6,681,165	23.27	9,858,108	28.93	11,451,297	23.32
2. Soybeans	171,000	0.60	1,318,809	3.87	8,774,023	17.87
3. Rice	2,965,684	10.33	4,979,165	14.61	6,243,138	12.71
4. Beans	2,560,281	8.92	3,484,778	10.22	4,643,409	9.46
5. Cotton	2,930,361	10.21	4,298,573	12.61	3,699,495	7.53
6. Sugar	1,339,933	4.67	1,725,121	5.06	2,607,628	5.31
7. Wheat	1,141,015	3.97	1,895,249	5.56	3,122,107	6.36
8. Cassava	1,342,403	4.68	2,024,557	5.94	2,015,857	4.11
9. Coffee	4,419,537	15.39	2,402,993	7.05	2,433,604	4.96
10. Oranges	112,241	0.39	202,037	0.59	575,249	1.17
11. Cacau	470,806	1.64	443,916	1.30	482,521	0.98
12. Tobacco	213,203	0.74	245,207	0.72	316,427	0.64
TOTALS[2]	24,347,629	84.80	32,878,513	96.47	46,364,755	94.42

Arable	28,712,209	100.00	34,081,443	100.00	49,104,263	100.00
Pasture	122,335,386		154,138,529		174,499,641	
Fallow	28,174,779		33,410,460		8,619,696	
Forest	57,945,105		57,881,182		88,167,703	
Other	12,694,663		14,633,852		24,796,570	
TOTALS	249,862,142		294,145,466		345,187,873	

[1] Ranked in order of total area (1982).
[2] Totals may vary because of because of double cropping
Source: Calculated from Anuario Estatistico (various years);
        Censo Agropecuario--IBGE (various years).

Examining, on the same basis, similar figures for the two main soybean states (Tables 5-9 and 5-10 for Rio Grande do Sul, and Tables 5-11 and 5-12 for Parana), the evidence is even clearer. However, in this case there were absolute as well as relative declines for most domestic staple crops. Between 1970 and 1980, in Rio Grande do Sul there were declines in the areas planted for all main staples with the exception of rice which increased by 37 percent; and in Parana all four declined. Tables 5-12 and 5-13 show that the increase in soybeans came at the expense of half a million hectares of domestic staples in Rio Grande do Sul, and nearly 400,000 in Parana.

On examining the situation on the frontier, a similar picture emerges. In Mato Gross do Sul, the former section of the state of Mato Grosso which is a heavy producer of soybeans, and where the soybean expansion came much later, the arable area increased from 1.27 million to 1.64 million hectares over the five year period 1975-1980 and the soybean area from 122,000 to 607,000 hectares (see Table 5-13). Nevertheless there was an absolute decline in the areas of rice and cassava, and beans and corn showed only a modest growth.

Table 5-9   Rio Grande do Sul:
Significant Crops, 1970 and 1980
(Hectares)

Crop[1]	1970	%	1980	%	% Change
Soybeans	1,600,131	32.14	3,763,073	56.31	135.17
Corn	1,870,469	37.57	1,557,904	23.31	(16.71)
Wheat	1,672,351	33.59	1,283,417	19.21	(23.26)
Rice	451,261	9.06	622,162	9.31	37.87
Black Beans	206,657	4.15	178,223	2.67	(13.76)
Cassava	251,945	5.06	111,642	1.67	(55.69)
Tobacco	88,191	1.77	101,358	1.52	14.93
Potatoes	106,430	2.14	86,435	1.29	(18.79)
Sugar Cane	41,732	0.84	32,193	0.48	(22.86)
Oranges	18,517	0.37	22,931	0.34	23.84
Peanuts	17,040	0.34	6,715	0.10	(60.59)
Totals[2]	6,324,724	127.05	7,766,053	116.21	
Total Arable Land	4,978,173	100.00	6,682,613	100.00	34.24
Pasture	14,634,986		13,302,315		(9.11)
Total Farm Area	23,807,179		24,057,610		1.05

[1] Ranked in order of total planting 1980
[2] Crop totals may add up to more than this figure because of double cropping.
Source: Censo Agropecuario--1970 and 1980.

Table 5-10   Rio Grande do Sul:
              Soybean Expansion and Changes in Domestic Staple Plantings,
                      Arable Land and Pasture, 1970 and 1980

Crop	1970	1980	Absolute Change
Potatoes	106,430	86,435	(19,995)
Black Beans	206,657	178,223	(28,434)
Cassava	251,945	111,642	(140,303)
Corn	1,870,469	1,557,904	(312,565)
	2,435,501	1,934,204	(501,297)
Soybeans	1,600,131	3,763,073	2,162,942
Total Arable[1]	4,978,173	6,682,613	1,704,440
Pasture	14,634,986	13,302,315	(1,332,671)

[1] Crop totals may add up to more than this figure because of
  double cropping.
Source: Censo Agropecuario—1970 and 1980.

Table 5-11   Parana:
              Significant Crops as a Percentage of Arable Land, 1970 and 1980

Crop[1]	1970	%	1980	%	% Change
Soybeans	395,484	8.38	2,075,657	34.11	424.84
Corn	2,122,206	44.98	1,862,670	30.61	(12.23)
Wheat	250,213	5.30	1,135,263	18.66	353.72
Black Beans	926,975	19.65	850,775	13.98	(8.22)
Coffee	360,896	7.65	677,299	11.13	87.67
Rice	441,645	9.36	342,600	5.63	(22.43)
Cotton	373,287	7.91	305,790	5.03	(18.08)
Sugar Cane	30,035	0.64	62,092	1.02	106.73
Cassava	87,445	1.85	46,726	0.77	(46.57)
Potatoes	25,932	0.55	39,146	0.64	50.96
Peanuts	110,167	2.33	28,861	0.47	(73.80)
Sub-total	5,124,285	109	7,426,879	122	44.93
Total Arable[2]	4,718,606	100.00	6,085,021	100.00	28.96
Pasture	4,509,710		5,520,218		22.41
Total Farm Area	14,625,530		16,380,332		12.00

[1] Ranked in order of total plantings 1980.
[2] Crop totals may add up to more than this figure because of
  double cropping.
Source: Censo Agropecuario—1970 and 1980.

Table 5-12   Parana:
            Soybean expansion and changes in Domestic Staple
                  Plantings, Arable Land and Pasture,
                            1970 and 1980

Crop	1970	1980	Absolute Change
Potatoes	25,932	39,146	13,214
Black Beans	926,975	850,775	(76,200)
Cassava	87,445	46,726	(40,719)
Corn	2,122,206	1,862,670	(259,536)
	3,162,558	2,799,317	(363,241)
Soybeans	395,484	2,075,657	1,680,173
Total Arable	4,718,606	6,085,021	1,366,415
Pasture	4,509,710	5,520,218	1,010,508

Source: Censo Agropecuario, 1970-80.

Table 5-13   Mato Grosso do Sul:
              Land Use - Significant Crops, 1975-80
                            (hectares)

Crop	1975	% of Arable Land	1980	% of Arable Land	% Change
Soybeans	121,829	9.56	606,998	36.97	79.93
Rice	595,454	46.72	347,561	21.17	-71.32
Corn	104,163	8.17	115,175	7.01	9.56
Wheat			76,978	4.69	
Beans	17,501	1.37	37,325	2.27	53.11
Cotton	26,028	2.04	33,882	2.06	23.18
Peanuts	22,698	1.78	15,266	0.93	-48.68
Sugar			9,547	0.58	
Cassava	5,804	0.46	5,017	0.31	-15.69
Total	893,477		1,247,749		
Arable	1,274,627		1,642,001		22.37
Pasture	20,793,497		21,334,938		2.54
Fallow	37,594		140,057		73.16
Forest & Woodland	4,139,900		4,651,260		10.99
Other	1,063,020		839,809		-26.58
Total	27,308,638		28,608,065		

Source: Censo Agropecuario, 1975 and 1980.

Significant for the nation as a whole is the overall production of domestic staples per head of the population. Tables for these crops are included in the Appendix. Tables A5-1, A5-3, A5-5, and A5-7, show Brazil's annual production of the four major domestic staples over the period 1960-1982. Also shown is Brazil's population over the same period, and production per capita for each of the crops. In the cases of cassava and beans--both important constituents in the diet of the population in the North and Northeast--total production has risen over the period. However, production per head of both crops has fallen. Tables A5-2 and A5-4 show the changes in production of each crop in index form, and make the picture even clearer. The index for both has fallen, but significantly, the decline for the most part clearly commenced in the 1970s and coincided with the soybean expansion.

Tables A5-6 and A5-8 show, the same computation for rice and corn. In the case of rice, there was a marginal increase in output per head. Only corn showed any significant growth. These figures suggest that in all four cases, with the exception of corn, yields have been a problem. It is likely that there was some substitution of soybeans for domestic staples on some of the higher quality land, particularly in Parana and Rio Grande do Sul. This would have had a proportionally larger effect upon national production. However, the figures also suggest that there was not the technical improvement that might have been expected over such a period, and this had a heavy impact on overall output. This will be discussed in the next section.

TECHNOLOGY

Intensification

In the last section, the area expansion and distribution of growth of the soybean crop in Brazil and in the main soybean growing states was analyzed. A further question of great importance is the degree to which the growth in output of soybeans was based either on area expansion or, on the other hand, on technological improvement through improved varieties, use of modern inputs, and improved husbandry techniques.

As suggested elsewhere, much of the encouragement for soybean expansion came through direct or indirect policy initiatives and favorable international price levels. However, these were not the necessarily the principal factors supporting the initial expansion of soybeans in Brazil.

During the 1960s, international prices remained virtually
constant in terms of nominal dollars yet there was an
increase of over 2 million hectares in area planted. In
addition, several other crops had price increases in the
1970s but none of them achieved growth rates such as those
achieved by soybeans (Homen de Melo, 1984).

Table 5-14   Annual Rates of Growth for Main Crops Showing
             Contribution of Area and Yield to Growth in Production

1962-82

Crop[1]	Production Growth Rate (%)	Area Growth Rate (%)	Contribution to Growth in Production(%)	Yield Growth Rate (%)	Contribution to Growth in Production(%)
1. Corn	5.59	1.40	25.04	4.19	74.96
2. Soybean	19.82	17.73	89.46	2.09	10.54
3. Rice	2.84	2.98	100.00	-0.14	0.00
4. Beans	2.69	3.97	100.00	-1.28	0.00
5. Cotton	0.00	0.24	100.00	-0.24	0.00
6. Sugar	5.61	3.78	67.38	1.83	32.62
7. Wheat	0.43	6.90	100.00	-6.47	0.00
8. Cassava	0.96	1.84	100.00	-0.87	0.00
9. Coffee	-4.01	-4.16	0.00	0.15	0.00
10. Oranges	12.00	8.03	66.92	3.97	33.08
11. Cacao	-1.36	6.90	100.00	-8.26	0.00
12. Tobacco	11.52	10.82	93.92	0.70	6.08

[1] Ranked in order of total area (1982)
Source: Calculated from Anuario Estatistico, IRBG, Brazil.

    In terms of overall output growth, the soybean crop owed
most to the expansion in area, but part of this growth also
resulted from the availability of new varieties and the
increasing use of modern inputs. Table 5-14 disaggregates
the annual growth rates for Brazil's main crops into the
contribution of area and yield increases to output growth.
As Table 5-15 shows, soybeans maintained an annual growth
rate of 19.8 percent between 1962 and 1982. During this
period, area expansion amounted to an annual growth rate of
17.7 percent, whereas yield per hectare grew at a rate of
2.19 percent. Looking at the contribution of each to output,
one finds that area expansion contributed 89.5 percent and
yield growth 10.5 percent.
    Early agronomic research in Brazil varied widely in both
quality and quantity (Schuh, 1970, 227). In the early 1960s

there was already some basic research into soybean production taking place in Brazil (Hartwig, 1966) and contacts were already being established with some U.S. research institutes. In 1964, after the revolutionary change in government, the first major strides toward developing the Brazilian soybean industry were taken through the creation of the National Commission for Soybeans to coordinate the work that was going on. This was strengthened by the additional appointment of a U.S. technical advisor to the commission, and the creation of a joint U.S-Brazil research venture, including the dispatch of U.S. agronomists to the agricultural research center in Campinas, Sao Paulo (Hymowitz et al, 1968).

The primary result of this activity was the development of commercial soybean varieties at the research institute at Campinas, based on varieties of U.S. origin. The ability to readily transfer existing technology from outside--in this case from the United States--to Brazil, demonstrates the importance of international knowledge transfer in introducing technological change in a development situation. Brazil experienced a significant savings in research costs by utilizing research completed elsewhere. As recently as 1980, of the 48 recommended varieties, 26 originated from national research programs and 22 came from the United States (Homem de Melo, 1984).

These technological innovations, and the consequent reductions in production costs served as one of the main contributors to the vast expansion of the soybean crop in Brazil. This concentration of research on soybeans was, in turn, part of the reason for the significant changes in agricultural output, and in particular the relative decline in output of domestic crops. As Table 5-14 shows, three of the four major domestic crops actually suffered declining yields, as did two important export crops, cotton and cacao.

The growth in the use of modern inputs in Brazilian arable crops as represented by the consumption of fertilizers was heavily influenced by the degree of subsidized credit which was made available, together with the specific government policies described earlier. Table 5-15 shows the growth in consumption, and Table 5-16 shows growth in the use of individual nutrients. The increase is greatest in the consumption of phosphates, a major nutrient of soybeans.
From 1974, the Brazilian government sought to increase agricultural output by further substantial investment in agricultural research. Improvement in technical efficiency and the continuing growth in the use of modern technical inputs was a fundamental of the program instituted through the Brazilian Agricultural Research Enterprise (EMBRAPA).

Table 5-15   Estimated Fertilizer Consumption, 1970-80
                              (000 Metric Tons)

Year	Nitrogen	Phosphates	Potassium	Total
1970	275.9	415.9	306.7	998.5
1971	278.4	534.9	350.8	1164.1
1972	411.6	875.6	460.0	1747.2
1973	346.1	804.6	528.5	1679.2
1974	396.2	914.2	521.3	1831.7
1975	406.2	1013.8	557.6	1977.6
1976	498.3	1308.3	721.5	2528.1
1977	700.5	1545.5	962.9	3208.9
1978	707.6	1523.1	990.9	3221.6
1979	758.0	1567.0	1085.0	3410.0
1980	888.0	1849.0	1269.0	4006.0

Source: World Bank, 1979a.

Table 5-16   Growth of Fertilizer Consumption, 1970-80
                              (1970 = 100)

Year	Nitrogen	Phosphates	Potassium	Total
1970	100	100	100	100
1971	101	129	114	117
1972	149	211	150	175
1973	125	193	172	168
1974	144	220	170	183
1975	147	244	182	198
1976	181	315	235	253
1977	254	372	314	321
1978	256	366	323	323
1979	275	377	354	342
1980	322	445	414	401

Source: World Bank, 1979a.

A central research station was set up in the state of Parana for soybeans in particular. Results from plantings both here, and at other experimental stations were used as controls; farmers were supplied with information about technical inputs on the control plots, which they then could use as their targets.

Mechanization

Mechanization is normally associated with the rising cost of labor. In countries such as the United States, farm mechanization followed industrial growth, which in turn was closely coupled to increases in demand for labor in the modern sector. In nations where there was traditionally a large rural population, mechanization followed much later, particularly when industrialization began to gather momentum after World War II and industry began to draw labor from rural regions. Unlike other inputs, mechanization is most responsive to the relative changes in the price of capital and labor (Sanders and Ruttan, 1978). Where mechanization has been introduced in areas where labor is abundant and wage rates consequently low, it has usually been for specific reasons such as opening up new lands or improving yields.

Mechanization began to grow rapidly in the 1960s and 1970s as a direct result of government policies. Resources were diverted toward subsidizing tractors and more significantly, to supporting the domestic tractor industry. Consequently, they were therefore diverted away from other potential areas such as agronomic research intended to increase yields. One effect of the subsidization of tractors was to shift the comparative advantage from the Northeast, with its high rural population and low wage levels, to the more developed South. Likewise, there was a shift in comparative advantage from smaller to larger farms (Sanders, 1978).

There were very few tractors in Brazil prior to the 1960s--a total of 8,372 in 1950, rising to 55,300 in 1960-- but since 1960 the numbers began increasing rapidly. They grew by a multiple of nearly 3 between 1960 and 1970, and by 3.5 between 1970 and 1980 (see Table 5-17). The government encouraged tractor purchase in a number of ways, including preferential exchange rates in the early years, although the main support was through subsidized rural credit loans with negative rates of interest and long periods of repayment. In reducing the price of capital in this way, the government presumed to encourage mechanization in those areas and upon

Table 5-17   Mechanization: Tractors and Area Planted,
                              1960-80

Year	Tractors[1] (000)	Area Planted	Ha/Tractor
Brazil			
1960	55,300	28,712,000	519
1970	146,300	34,081,443	233
1975	284,500	33,803,000	119
1980	517,638	49,104,263	95
Rio Grande do Sul			
1970	39,993	4,979,129	125
1975	77,254	5,925,382	77
1980	114,774	6,682,613	58
Parana			
1970	16,052	4,718,606	294
1975	50,003	5,627,535	113
1980	78,325	6,085,021	78

[1]Over 10 HP
Source: World Bank, 1979; Censo Agropecuario;
              Soskin,1981.

those farms where the supply of rural credit was available.
There was a substantially favorable weighting toward loans to
larger farms, farms in the South, and soybean growers.
Hence it follows that the subsidized credit provided a spur
to mechanization and would have encouraged the replacement of
labor. The scale of many of the farms in the South and the
type of soybean technology which was available were stimuli
toward mechanized production.

This is supported by the data in Table 5-18 which shows
the distribution of tractors within Brazil together with the
number of tractors per 1,000 agricultural workers. There was
a dramatic rise in tractors in Rio Grande do Sul between 1970
and 1980 (187 percent), with the increase in the same period
in Parana amounting to 388 percent. This represented annual
growth rates of 11 and 17 percent, respectively. Further
evidence is available to show how area-specific the increase
in mechanization was within Rio Grande do Sul, the increases
heavily favored the regions with the highest concentration of
soybean plantings (Soskin, 1981).

Table 5-18   Brazil: Distribution of Tractors, 1960-80

State	Percentage of Brazil's Tractor Stock			Tractors per 1000 Agricultural Workers		
	1960	1970	1980	1960	1970	1980
South:						
Parana	8.4	11.2	15.0	4.0	9.4	45.2
Santa Catarina	1.8	3.7	6.1	1.9	7.9	39.6
Rio Grande do Sul	24.7	24.1	22.0	11.4	27.6	111.5
North & Northeast	7.6	7.3	8.1	n.a	n.a	4.0
Southeast:						
Minas Gerais	7.8	5.6	9.1	2.3	4.4	21.6
Espirito Santo	n.s	n.s	1.0	n.a	n.a	15.3
Rio de Janeiro	2.7	2.3	1.7	6.3	15.7	30.1
Sao Paulo	44.3	39.6	25.4	15.7	43.5	100.8
Center-West	2.7	6.2	11.6	7.2	22.2	27.5
BRAZIL	100.0	100.0	100.0			

Source: Data for 1960-70: Sanders, 1978; 1980: Censo Agropecuario.

Rural Employment

Regional disparities in population distribution and employment opportunities havè long been characteristics of Brazilian economic development. "Brazil has experienced a common trait of economic history, the polarization of growth where newly developing areas sucked the skills, capital and entrepreneurship from regions where early development took place" (Lewis 1979). This was very much the case with the decline in economic importance of Northeast Brazil which came as the center of growth moved to the developing industrial areas further south, leaving in its wake the legacy of a large, poor rural population with limited possibilities of reaping the benefits accruing to the new industrial centers.

The implications of this historic distribution of population are apparent from Table 5-19. The Northeast, with 30 percent of Brazil's total population in 1970, had 40 percent of the rural population; ten years later the area's share of the total population had fallen marginally to 29 percent, but

Table 5-19   Brazil: Rural and Urban Population, 1970 and 1980

Region	1970					1980				
	Urban	Rural	%	Total	% Rural	Urban	Rural	%	Total	% Rural
North	1,626,600	1,977,260	4.8	3,603,860	54.9	3,046,129	2,847,007	7.4	5,893,136	48.3
Northeast	11,752,977	16,358,950	39.8	28,111,927	58.2	17,585,618	17,276,289	44.7	34,861,907	49.6
Southeast	28,964,601	10,888,897	26.5	39,853,498	27.3	42,848,823	8,903,828	23.1	51,752,651	17.2
South	7,303,427	9,193,066	22.4	16,496,493	55.7	11,880,533	7,155,896	18.5	19,036,429	37.6
Center-West	2,437,379	2,635,880	6.4	5,073,259	52.0	5,118,092	2,436,777	6.3	7,554,869	32.3
BRAZIL	52,084,984	41,054,053	100.0	93,139,037	44.1	80,479,195	38,619,797	100.0	119,098,992	32.4

Source: Crescimento e Distribuicao da Populacao Brasileira, 1940-80; IBGE--Rio de Janeiro, 1980.

Table 5-20   Brazil: Changes in Population, 1970-80

Region	Urban % Change	Annual Rate	Rural % Change	Annual Rate	Total % Change	Annual Rate
North	46.6	6.5	44.0	3.7	63.5	5.0
Northeast	33.2	4.1	5.6	0.5	24.0	2.2
Southeast	32.4	4.0	-18.2	-2.0	29.9	2.6
South	38.5	5.0	-22.2	-2.5	15.4	1.4
Center-West	52.4	7.7	-7.6	-0.8	48.9	4.1
BRAZIL	35.3	4.4	-5.9	-0.6	27.9	2.5

Source: Crescimento e Distribuicao da Populacao Brasileira,
1940-80--IBGE--Rio de Janiero--1980.

its share of the total rural population had risen to nearly
45 percent. However, even with this relatively high dependence on rural employment, there was no consequent effort on
the part of the Brazilian government to divert resources
specifically designated for agricultural development to that
area.
    The trends and rates of change in the distribution of
population are shown in Table 5-20. Whereas Brazil's rural
population fell by 5.9 percent between 1970 and 1980, all the
losses came from the southeast, (with its high industrial
growth) and the rapidly developing agricultural centers in
the South and Center-West. Both the North, and Northeast
showed actual increases in rural population.

Table 5-21   Rio Grande do Sul: Urban & Rural Population,
                                 1960-80

	1960 Population	%	1970 Population	%	1980 Population	%	Rate of Growth (%) 1960-70	1970-80
Urban	2,380,783	44.4	3,553,006	53.3	5,252,465	67.5	4.08	3.99
Rural	2,985,937	55.6	3,111,880	46.7	2,524,747	32.5	0.41	-2.07
Total	5,366,720	100.0	6,664,886	100.0	7,777,212	100.0	2.19	1.56

Source: Crescimento e Distribuicao da Populacao Brasileira, 1940-80;
        IBGE--Rio de Janeiro, 1980.

Table 5-22   Parana: Urban & Rural Population,

1960-80

| | 1960 | | 1970 | | 1980 | | Rate of Growth (%) | |
	Population	%	Population	%	Population	%	1960-70	1970-80
Urban	1,438,018	26.8	2,504,378	37.6	4,473,541	57.5	5.70	5.97
Rural	3,082,517	57.4	4,425,490	66.4	3,156,925	40.6	3.68	-3.32
Total	4,520,535	84.2	6,929,868	104.0	7,630,466	98.1	4.36	0.97

Source: Crescimento e Distribuicao da Populacao Brasileira, 1940-80;
        IBGE--Rio de Janeiro, 1980.

The data from the two main soybean states in Table 5-21 shows that while in the period 1960-1970, the rural population increased by an annual rate of .41 percent in Rio Grande Do Sul and 3.68 percent in Parana, in the subsequent decade the rural population fell by 2.07 percent and 3.32 percent respectively.

The sections above have established that the growth of the soybean acreage was highly area-specific and--especially in the 1970s--was closely associated with mechanized agriculture. It also appears clear from the population changes that the high concentration of soybeans in the two states contributed to the release of labor and therefore to the decline in rural employment.

6
Micro Impact—
Secondary Production

Development

The soybean crushing industry has long been a significant factor within the Brazilian soybean complex. From the early years of the soybean expansion, soybeans were crushed in small or medium-sized plants, which were family-owned and originally designed to crush other oil seeds such as cotton-seed, peanuts, or castor beans, and only latterly adapted to soybean crushing (Thompson, 1979). During the 1950s and 1960s, the absolute tonnage crushed remained small, but by 1958, however, in excess of 50 percent of the domestic crop was being crushed in Brazil. Table 6-1 sets out the crush in relation to total domestic supply from 1960 until 1982. Both the crush and crushing capacity began to grow substantially at the latter end of the 1960s (see Table 6-2), with the crush passing the one-million metric ton mark in 1970, when it contributed some 68 percent of Brazilian production. By 1977 the crush had mushroomed to close to nine million tons, representing virtually 70 percent of production, and Brazil had by then 12.5 million tons of crushing capacity.

There appears to be very limited data on the number and sizes of soybeans crushing firms in Brazil during the early years, but Table 6-3 gives an indication of the number and distribution of firms in 1977. The total daily capacity of about 40,500 metric tons gives an annual capacity of just under 11 million tons based on a working year of 270 days. As

Table 6-1 Brazilian Soybean Output and Crush, 1960-82
(Million Metric Tons)

Year	Output	Export	%	Other[1]	Crush	%
1960	206	0	0.0	74	132	64.1
1961	271	73	26.9	55	143	52.8
1962	345	97	28.1	75	173	50.1
1963	323	34	10.5	89	200	61.9
1964	305	0	0.0	75	227	74.4
1965	523	75	14.3	149	289	55.3
1966	595	121	20.3	64	404	67.9
1967	716	305	42.6	74	335	46.8
1968	654	66	10.1	88	493	75.4
1969	1057	310	29.3	105	630	59.6
1970	1508	290	19.2	150	1025	68.0
1971	2077	296	14.3	200	1600	77.0
1972	3223	1024	31.8	331	2326	72.2
1973	5012	1788	35.7	474	2651	52.9
1974	7876	2863	36.4	685	4267	54.2
1975	9893	3516	35.5	880	5279	53.4
1976	11223	3352	29.9	925	6781	60.4
1977	12513	2581	20.6	1090	8661	69.2
1978	9541	659	6.9	838	8882	93.1
1979	10240	638	6.2	895	9094	88.8
1980	15156	1533	10.1	920	13009	85.8
1981	15200	1502	9.9	890	13796	90.8
1982	12835	797	6.2	895	12728	99.2

1Other includes seed and waste.
Totals might exceed 100 percent because of imports.
Source: FAO Production Yearbook; Anuario Estatistico;
World Bank, 1979a.

shown in the table, of the 132 plants, 110 had capacities of less than 500 tons per day. The traditional crushing industry was centered in the state of Sao Paulo, where 41 percent of the plants were to be found, although they actually crushed less than 25 percent of the total. However, the largest specialist soybean crushers had already appeared in what had become the center of Brazilian soybean production, Rio Grande do Sul and the neighboring state of Parana. In this region eight out of the total of nine plants had a capacity in excess of 1000 tons. Together with the 58 smaller plants in these two states, these were processing

over 68 percent of the total crush. Along with Sao Paulo
these three states held 93 percent of the crush capacity.

Table 6-2   Soybean Crush Capacity and Utilization
                            (000 Metric Tons)

Year	Production	Crush Capacity	Ratio of Capacity to Production	Domestic Crush	Capacity Utilzed(%)	Proportion Crushed(%)
1969	1,057	775	0.73	641	60.64	73.32
1971	2,077	2,040	0.98	1,600	77.03	98.22
1973	5,012	3,306	0.66	2,651	52.89	65.96
1975	9,893	6,200	0.63	5,279	53.36	62.67
1977	12,513	2,000	0.96	8,661	69.22	95.90
1979	10,240	5,000	1.46	9,094	88.81	146.48
1981	15,200	18,000	1.18	13,796	90.76	118.42
1983	15,200	21,000	1.38	12,510	82.30	138.16

Source: FAO Production Year Book; Annuario Estatistico;
        Gulliver, 1981; Drefus et Cie, 1984).

A study in Brazil in 1977 suggested that the older,
smaller firms tended to be inefficient, operating with
outdated plant and very limited working capital (Thompson,
1979). Many of these plants actually had to halt operations
for a large part of the year because of the lack of resources
to purchase soybeans in the period between harvests. The
larger operators were able to maintain operations throughout
the year, with an average idle period of only 30 days,
because of their greater financial resources which allowed
them greater freedom in the purchase and holding of stocks.
By the late 1970s, larger plants, capable of crushing between
1200 and 2000 tons per day, were being constructed. This
period saw a rapid increase in the number of multinationals,
and by 1978 it was estimated that one third of the total
capacity was owned by multinationals, fifteen percent by
cooperatives, and the remainder by private firms. Within the
private sector, the facilities were for the most part family-
owned and operated (Gulliver, 1981). Large, modern plants
operate at around 85 percent capacity based on a 270 to 300
day working year. Traditionally, Brazilian crushing plants
were based on the batch extraction system, which lends itself
to processing a variety of oil seeds. The modern plants for
the most part use the solvent extraction system which has

considerable advantages with low oil content seeds such as soybeans. The solvent extraction process requires approximately half the labor and energy of the batch system. This gives the larger operators of modern plants a considerable cost advantage over the more traditional plants.

Table 6-3   Soybean Crushing Capacity by Size of Firm in Four States,
Brazil, 1977
(Capacity in Metric Tons per Day)

State	0-499		500-999		More than 1000		State Totals	
	Firms and Crush Capacity	Percent of State Capacity	Firms and Crush Capacity	Percent of State Capacity	Firms and Crush Capacity	Percent of State Capacity	Firms and Crush Capacity	Percent of Brazil Capacity
Rio Grande do Sul	25 3,822	24	6 4,320	28	5 7,500	48	36 15,642	39
Parana	23 4,342	36	4 2,600	22	3 5,150	43	30 12,092	30
Santa Catarina	8 1,520	72	1 600	28			9 2,120	5
Mias Gerais	3 585	100					3 585	1
Total Firms (Brazil) Crush Capacity	110 17,614	43	13 8,920	22	9 14,000	35	132 40,534	

Source: Thompson, 1979.

Structure of the Industry

By the early 1980s, the situation had changed dramatically. Total capacity had almost doubled, from just under 11 million tons to over 20 million tons per annum, or from 40,500 tons per day to over 75,000 tons (Drefus et Cie, 1984). In addition, the industry went through a period of considerable modernization and rationalization. It is estimated that by 1984 only 76 operating plants remained, and of these almost half had a capacity of over 1500 tons per day. (It must be assumed that by this time these figures left out the very small plants, which were primarily concerned with processing other oil seeds.)

Of the total industry capacity in 1984, 22 percent was by then owned and operated by multinational companies, 15 percent by cooperatives, and the remaining 63 percent by private Brazilian firms, with almost half of these being substantial Brazilian operations with capacities of over 2000 tons per day. The capacity had, therefore, virtually doubled since the mid-1970s. In addition, the industry went through a modernization process which resulted in about half the capacity now being capable of outputs of 1500 million tons a day, against only a fifth less than a decade earlier.

The utilization of crush capacity is estimated to be around 65 percent. The breakdown of the capacity between states in 1984 is shown in Table 6-4. Brazil traditionally has had a geographically concentrated crushing industry, and although a substantial amount of new capacity was constructed, the majority of the plants remain in the traditional areas.

Table 6-4 Breakdown of Crushing Capacity by State, 1983
(Million Metric Tons)

State	Capacity	%
Sao Paulo	2.9	14.38
Parana	7.4	36.69
Santa Caterina	1.36	6.74
Rio Grande do Sul	8.1	40.16
Others	0.41	2.03
BRAZIL	20.17	100

Source: Drefus et Cie, 1984.

What was the reason for this sudden and very dramatic increase in crushing capacity? First, the expansion of crushing capacity did, to a degree, follow the expansion of soybean production as a whole. However, as demonstrated in Table 6-2, starting in 1978, Brazil's crushing capacity began to grow at a far faster rate than soybean output. This appears to indicate a conscious change in the policy environment, which reflected the Brazilian government's desire to retain the added value on the product within Brazil. Substantial taxation was levied on raw beans, this acted as a deterrent to whole bean exports. In fact, soybean exports fell as a percentage of total production from 36 percent in 1975 to 6.2 percent in 1982. At the same time exports of oil increased to around 40 percent of production and exports of meal to 80 percent.

Second, the government allowed crushers to reap very considerable benefits from heavily subsidized rural credit, not only for the construction of fixed plant, but also for working capital. This significantly helped to finance

crushers in purchasing and storing soybeans and was eventually even reflected in imports of whole beans for processing in
Brazil when the Brazilian capacity began to exceed domestic
supply. The availability of subsidized credit proved a
considerable attraction to the giant multinational traders,
and by the early 1980s over 20 percent of Brazilian crushing
capacity was in their hands. It remains unlikely that in the
absence of strong financial incentives, neither this substantial growth in crushing capacity nor the participation of
the multinational companies would have occurred to such a
great extent. (Drefus et Cie., 1984).

However, as attractive as the subsidized credit might
have been, ultimately the decision to construct new plant
will depend on the profitability of soybean crushing in
Brazil. This, in turn, depends upon the "soybean-crushing
margin," or the net figure obtained by the crusher for the
product of the crush, less the price of the beans. Gulliver
suggested that calculating the implicit margin in this way
(using the f.o.b export price as the price of beans), and
calculating for refined or crude oil (by making the appropriate adjustment to the oil yield factor) domestic crushing
showed positive crushing margins in 1974, assuming the
production of crude oil. With refined oil in the calc-
ulation, the margins were positive for each year except 1973

Table 6-5   Implicit Crush Margins, 1970-77
        Export Prices of Soybeans, Soymeal and Soyoil, F.O.B.
                      ($ per Metric Ton)

Year	Beans	Meal	Oil Refined	Oil Crude	Implicit Crush Margin Refined[1]	Implicit Crush Margin Crude[2]
1970	93.50	83.08	28.62	–	20.15	–
1971	113.90	89.46	336.62	–	13.00	–
1972	123.33	108.41	244.54	–	1.86	–
1973	276.66	267.24	297.37	387.71	-21.52	-1.83
1974	214.72	149.21	750.00	830.04	29.93	52.24
1975	205.47	148.55	886.40	579.22	62.55	14.58
1976	216.33	181.38	492.20	385.62	7.65	-7.14
1977	274.56	214.66	617.40	562.66	-3.36	-7.33

[1] Calculated as 0.76 times meal price plus 0.175 times refined oil price
  less bean price.
[2] Calculated as 0.76 times meal price plus 0.85 times crude oil price
  less bean price.
Source: Gulliver, 1981.

and 1977 using the f.o.b export price as the opportunity cost of domestic crushing (see Table 6-5). Gulliver's calculations showed that between 1973 and 1977, domestic crushing was unprofitable in three out of the five years, implying that if there had been a negative export margin, then the government had had to intervene to make the internal crush margin positive in those years (Gulliver, 1981).

Employment

The effect on employment of the construction of such a large soybean crushing capacity within Brazil is only the subject of conjecture, since no specific figures are available. The construction of the plants themselves obviously had a positive impact on employment in the construction and mechanical engineering industries. The impact on employment through the operation of these plants was positive but small. The modern plants, although employing more man-power per hour of operation than similar U.S. plants, were capital intensive, with a limited labor requirement. The older plants, being situated in largely rural areas, did have some beneficial effect on employment.

Domestic Product Demand

One considerable benefit to the general population from the development of the Brazilian domestic crushing industry was the increasing availability of soybean oil, and subsequently soybean meal. Table 6-6 shows the dramatic growth of domestic consumption of both oil and meal between 1960 and 1982. The domestic consumption of oil grew at an annual rate of over 21 percent, and meal consumption grew at almost 15 percent.

Crude soybean oil has limited industrial uses in Brazil. To some extent it is used in the manufacture of plastics and paint, however, the majority is further refined to produce cooking oil or for inclusion in, or for the manufacture of, other food products. There is a substantial level of integration within the soybean processing industry, with many of the larger crushers also refining and canning. It would seem that this level of integration is necessary for profitability. There is a further reason for integration, as by law, firms may not export soy oil unless they also sell it on the domestic market (Gulliver, 1981).

Table 6-6   Domestic Consumption of Soybean oil and
Meal, Brazil 1960-82

Year	(000 Metric Tons) Meal	Oil
1960	98	22
1961	106	26
1962	129	33
1963	88	36
1964	128	42
1965	119	61
1966	123	82
1967	140	77
1968	139	89
1969	105	113
1970	173	194
1971	251	282
1972	248	372
1973	603	397
1974	718	694
1975	840	682
1976	970	850
1977	1438	1025
1978	1461	1110
1979	1971	1309
1980	2595	1516
1981	2271	1490
1982	1956	1505

Source: FAO Trade Year Book, USDA Data.

In the food industry the major use of refined soybean oil is for the manufacture of margarine, and cooking oils. Soybean oil is the major component of Brazilian margarine. Since 1960 there has been a considerable level of substitution of soybean oil for the traditionally used peanut and cotton seed oils (Table 6-7).

Soybean oil is heavily used in urban areas and its consumption increased with the urbanization of Brazil and growing incomes. By the 1970s the population had become heavily dependant on soybean oil; its availability and price levels assumed considerable political significance. Traditionally, lard was the other major component of the edible oil market and Gulliver suggests that it is reasonable to assume that there was also some substitution between soybean oil and lard. (Gulliver, 1981)).

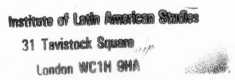

Table 6-7   Apparent Consumption of Edible Vegatable Oil,
Brazil, 1960-78

Year	Soybean Oil[1]	Peanut Oil	Cottonseed Oil	Total	% Soybean Oil
1960	22	112	87	221	9.95
1961	26	159	108	293	8.87
1962	33	168	128	329	10.03
1963	36	151	119	306	11.76
1964	42	128	127	297	14.14
1965	61	198	103	362	16.85
1966	82	240	128	450	18.22
1967	77	193	103	373	20.64
1968	89	203	130	422	21.09
1969	113	197	168	478	23.64
1970	194	206	140	540	35.93
1971	282	248	121	651	43.32
1972	372	167	170	709	52.47
1973	397	101	150	648	61.27
1974	694	72	132	898	77.28
1975	682	65	N/A	747	91.30
1976	850	40	N/A	890	95.51
1977	1,025	16	113	1,154	88.82
1978	1,110	10	128	1,248	88.94

Source: [1] FAO   Trade Year Book (various Issues),
U.N., Rome; remainder Gulliver, 1981.

At the time of the food crisis of 1964, soybean oil was one of the food products on which price ceilings had been imposed in the battle against inflation.   Later, price control and government interference in the soybean oil market has remained a feature of Brazilian policy.   Price controls maintained domestic prices below the world price, resulting in the introduction of embargoes on exports.   The net result was domestic oil shortages.

Following the growth of the crushing industry and the growing domestic demand for soybean oil came increasing demand for soybean meal.   Soybean meal consumption in 1970 was less than 175 thousand metric tons, and had grown to more than 2.5 million metric tons by 1980.   As might be expected, with Brazilian per capita incomes rising, the demand for animal products expanded.   The net result was the modernization and rapid growth of the Brazilian poultry industry.

Poultry rations account for around 75 percent of the domestic soybean meal consumption. The growth in the Brazil-

Table 6-8   Poultry Meat Production and Consumption,
Brazil, 1964-83
(000 Metric Tons)

Year	Product-ion	Exports	Consump-tion	Population Brazil[1] (Millions)	Consumption Per Head(Kg)
1964	94	0	94	78.73	1.2
1965	99	0	99	81.01	1.2
1966	104	0	104	82.93	1.3
1967	109	0	109	85.24	1.3
1968	122	0	122	87.62	1.4
1969	190	n.a.	190	90.07	2.1
1970	192	n.a.	192	92.52	2.1
1971	336	n.a.	336	95.17	3.5
1972	357	n.a.	357	97.85	3.6
1973	381	n.a.	381	100.56	3.8
1974	369	n.a.	369	103.35	3.6
1975	586	n.a.	586	106.23	5.5
1976	641	n.a.	641	107.54	6.0
1977	680	n.a.	680	110.21	6.2
1978	569	52	517	112.94	4.6
1979	1096	81	1015	115.74	8.8
1980	1326	170	1156	121.29	9.5
1981	1491	296	1195	124.02	9.6
1982	1596	302	1294	126.81	10.2
1983	1580	239	1341	129.66	10.3

Source: Oil World; FAO Trade Year Book; USDA FAS Data,
[1] IMF--International Financial Statistics.

ian poultry industry was, to an extent, reflected in the increase in egg production, but more important was the production of poultry meat.   Total output of poultry meat more than tripled between 1964 and 1971, and then nearly quintupled between 1971 and 1982 when total output reached nearly 1.6 million tons. Table 6-8 demonstrates this rapid expansion, and also shows the increases in consumption of poultry meat per head of the Brazilian population.   Consumption per head rose from 1.2 kilograms per head per annum in 1964, to 10.2 kilograms in 1982.

This new supply of animal products became increasingly important in Brazil and was a direct result of the substantial investment in the domestic crushing capacity. Furthermore, by the late 1970s Brazil was able to develop a valuable export market for poultry meat especially in the Middle East.

7
Soybean Expansion –
Macro Impact

BALANCE OF PAYMENTS

The period 1960-1980 was a time of strong economic growth for Brazil, particularly during the second decade. It was this latter period that included the so-called "miracle years" of Brazilian economic expansion. Real growth picked up fiercely during the 1960s, particularly toward the end of the decade, in spite of rising inflation. The economy achieved a compound rate of expansion of around 6.2 percent during the period. Tables 7-1 and 7-2 give some idea of the figures involved. Although agriculture was to fall in terms of its contribution to the whole economy, the sector showed continual expansion in absolute terms, growing at a rate of 7.8 percent during the first decade and 5.4 percent during the second.

It was through its contribution to Brazil's exports that agriculture was most conspicuously successful. Agricultural products came to represent the majority share of Brazil's exports. Coffee was the mainstay of these making up around 50 percent of the total. Soybeans made only a very small contribution until well into the 1970s, but by the middle of the decade the crop or its products overtook coffee as Brazil's major agricultural export. Table 7-3 illustrates the growth of economic activity and the change in proportions of each product group.

It was the oil crisis and the soaring costs of imported petroleum that had a severe impact on Brazil's balance of payments in the years from 1974 until 1980. This was a primary cause of Brazil's drive to encourage soybean production.

Table 7-1   Brazil Economic Performance:
Gross Domestic Product by Economic Activity at Factor Cost
(Millions of Cruzeiros at Current Prices)

Economic Activity	1960	1965	1970	1975	1978	1980	1982
Agriculture	503	5,834	20,157	107,349	469,396	1,649,091	5,320,637
Mining	10	287	1,350	6,022	22,231	39,096	366,093
Manufacture	483	9,092	46,619	263,087	919,904	3,412,793	12,396,214
Electricity, Gas & Water	39	608	3,402	16,555	50,866	176,474	813,644
Construction	33	1,946	9,658	61,661	194,001	628,446	2,847,616
Wholesale,Retail,Hotels	338	5,521	29,902	160,839	595,143	2,129,038	7,687,005
Transport	145	2,293	7,679	40,321	165,022	575,139	2,658,353
Financial & other Services, including Housing & Government Services	941	16,772	86,505	434,121	1,736,425	5,857,327	25,400,845
Less Imputed Bank Service Charges			(7,286)	(52,381)	(240,281)	(661,179)	(2,914,976)
TOTAL: GDP	2,491	42,351	197,987	1,037,574	3,912,705	13,806,225	54,575,431

(percentage contibution)

Economic Activity	1960	1965	1970	1975	1978	1980	1982
Agriculture	20.2	13.8	10.2	10.3	12.0	11.9	9.7
Mining	0.4	0.7	0.7	0.6	0.6	0.3	0.7
Manufacture	19.4	21.5	23.5	25.4	23.5	24.7	22.7
Electricity, Gas & Water	1.6	1.4	1.7	1.6	1.3	1.3	1.5
Construction	1.3	4.6	4.9	5.9	5.0	4.6	5.2
Wholesale,Retail,Hotels	13.6	13.0	15.1	15.5	15.2	15.4	14.1
Transport	5.8	5.4	3.9	3.9	4.2	4.2	4.9
Financial & other Services, including Housing & Government Services	37.8	39.6	43.7	41.8	44.4	42.4	46.5
Less Imputed Bank Service Charges	0.0	0.0	-3.7	-5.0	-6.1	-4.8	-5.3
TOTAL: GDP	100.0	100.0	100.0	100.0	100.0	100.0	100.0

Source: Calculated from IMF--Balance of Payments Year Book, various issues, IMF, Washington.
and Brazilian National Accounts.

The growing world demand for soybean products produced high
price levels and Brazil was able to take advantage of the
strong market. The pattern of Brazil's balance of payments
and the contribution of both soybeans and coffee are set out
in Table 7-4.

It is of importance to examine the import pattern at
this time. As a high technology crop with a high technical
input requirement, soybeans could well have led to substantial imports. Although imports of agricultural requisites

Table 7-2 Brazil Economic Performance:
Gross Domestic Product by Economic Activity at Factor Cost
(Millions of Cruzeiros at 1980 Prices)

GDP Deflator (1980 = 100)	3.4	10.7	32.6	100.0	388.5
Economic Activity	1970	1975	1978	1980	1982
Agriculture	592,853	1,003,260	1,439,866	1,649,091	1,369,533
Mining	39,712	56,284	68,192	39,096	94,233
Manufacture	1,371,138	2,458,755	2,821,790	3,412,793	3,190,789
Electricity, Gas & Water	100,062	154,720	156,030	176,474	209,432
Construction	284,053	576,269	595,094	628,446	732,977
Wholesale,Retail Trade, Resturants and Hotels	879,474	1,503,168	1,825,591	2,129,038	1,978,637
Transport	225,853	376,832	506,202	575,139	684,261
Financial & other Services, including Housing & Government Services	2,544,276	4,057,201	5,326,456	5,857,327	6,538,184
Less Imputed Bank Service Charges	(214,282)	(489,538)	(737,060)	(661,179)	(750,315)
TOTAL: GDP	5,823,138	9,696,951	12,002,162	13,806,225	14,047,730

(Indexed: 1970 = 100)

Economic Activity	1970	1975	1978	1980	1982
Agriculture	100.0	169.2	242.9	278.2	231.0
Mining	100.0	141.7	171.7	98.4	237.3
Manufacture	100.0	179.3	205.8	248.9	232.7
Electricity, Gas & Water	100.0	154.6	155.9	176.4	209.3
Construction	100.0	202.9	209.5	221.2	258.0
Wholesale,Retail Trade, Resturants and Hotels	100.0	170.9	207.6	242.1	225.0
Transport	100.0	166.8	224.1	254.7	303.0
Financial & other Services, including Housing & Government Services	100.0	159.5	209.4	230.2	257.0
Less Imputed Bank Service Charges	-100.0	-228.5	-344.0	-308.6	-350.2
TOTAL: GDP	100.0	166.5	206.1	237.1	241.2

Source: Calculated from IMF Balance of Payments Year Book, various issues, IMF, Washington; and Brazilian National Accounts.

rose over the period, their proportion to total imports remained constant at a fairly low figure, and fell rapidly in proportion to agricultural exports. One may conclude from this that soybeans did not require a substantial element of import content. Table 7-5 shows the structure of Brazil's imports, the element of agricultural products and the element of imported agricultural requisites.

Table 7-3

Brazil Trade Balance:
Structure of Exports, 1964-80
(in Millions of U.S. dollars)

	1964	1966	1968	1970	1972	1974	1976	1978	1980
Total Exports	1429.8	1741.4	1881.3	2738.9	3991.2	6199.2	10128.3	12658.9	20132.4
Agricultural Products	1185.0	1395.8	1489.8	1967.1	2743.1	4864.7	6142.6	6716.1	9420.9
Coffee	760.0	764.0	775.0	939.0	989.0	864.0	2173.0	1947.0	2486.0
Soybeans & Prods.	3.0	28.0	25.0	72.0	295.0	891.0	1780.0	1515.0	2264.0
Sugar	33.1	80.5	106.3	134.5	417.9	1386.5	182.3	465.2	1398.2
Other Ag. Prods	388.9	523.3	583.5	821.6	1041.2	1723.2	2007.3	2788.9	3272.7
Other Exports	244.8	345.6	391.5	771.8	1248.1	1334.5	3985.7	5942.8	10711.5

(in Percentage Proportions)

	1964	1966	1968	1970	1972	1974	1976	1978	1980
Total Exports	100.0	100.0	100.0	100.0	100.0	100.0	100.0	100.0	100.0
Agricultural Products	82.9	80.2	79.2	71.8	68.7	78.5	60.6	53.1	46.8
Coffee	53.2	43.9	41.2	34.3	24.8	13.9	21.5	15.4	12.3
Soybeans & Prods.	0.2	1.6	1.3	2.6	7.4	14.4	17.6	12.0	11.2
Sugar	2.3	4.6	5.7	4.9	10.5	22.4	1.8	3.7	6.9
Other Ag. Prods	27.2	30.1	31.0	30.0	26.1	27.8	.19.8	22.0	16.3
Other Exports	17.1	19.8	20.8	28.2	31.3	21.5	39.4	46.9	53.2

Source: FAO Trade Year Book (various issues); IMF Balance of Payments Year Book (various issues).

Table 7-4

Brazil   Trade Balance: 1960-82
(in millions of US dollars)

Year	Exports	Coffee	%	Soybeans & Prods.	%	Trade Balance (f.o.b.)
1960	1,268	713	56.2	0	0.0	(23)
1961	1,403	710	50.6	7	0.5	113
1962	1,214	643	53.0	8	0.7	−89
1963	1,406	748	53.2	7	0.5	112
1964	1,430	760	53.1	3	0.2	344
1965	1,596	707	44.3	15	0.9	655
1966	1,741	764	43.9	28	1.6	438
1967	1,654	705	42.6	39	2.4	213
1968	1,881	775	41.2	25	1.3	26
1969	2,311	813	35.2	53	2.3	318
1970	2,739	939	34.3	72	2.6	232
1971	2,904	773	26.6	108	3.7	(365)
1972	3,991	989	24.8	295	7.4	(252)
1973	6,199	1,244	20.1	949	15.3	(61)
1974	7,951	864	10.9	891	11.2	(4,748)
1975	8,670	855	9.9	1,304	15.0	(3,549)
1976	10,128	2,173	21.5	1,780	17.6	(2,385)
1977	12,120	2,299	19.0	2,143	17.7	(99)
1978	12,659	1,947	15.4	1,515	12.0	(1,156)
1979	15,244	1,918	12.6	1,650	10.8	(2,717)
1980	20,132	2,486	12.3	2,264	11.2	(2,823)
1981	23,293	1,517	6.5	3,191	13.7	1,185
1982	20,175	1,858	9.2	2,122	10.5	778

Source: IMF Balance of Payments Year Book (various issues).

Table 7-5
Brazil   Trade Balance:
Structure of Imports, 1964-80
(in Millions of U.S. Dollars)

	1964	1966	1968	1970	1972	1974	1976	1978	1980
Total Imports	1263.5	1496.2	2128.7	2849.2	4783.3	14167.9	13622.7	15054.3	24960.5
Agricultural Products	315.2	290.2	365.4	302.8	389.2	1128.5	1112.5	1546.0	2470.6
Agricultural Requisites	37.5	49.4	59.4	185.3	201.4	881.0	562.6	594.3	910.0
Crude Fertilizers	4.9	4.2	7.7	8.1	45.7	20.6	77.3	52.4	57.8
Manuf. Fertilizers	19.2	26.0	45.0	70.6	122.8	490.5	247.8	369.0	777.9
Pesticides	5.1	11.8	13.7	187.7	122.8	94.1	109.4	125.1	309.9
Agric. Machines	8.3	7.4	13.7	87.7	142.8	216.3	128.1	47.8	43.3
Other Imports	910.8	1156.6	1703.9	2361.2	4192.7	12158.4	11947.6	12914.0	21579.9

(in Percentage Proportions)

	1964	1966	1968	1970	1972	1974	1976	1978	1980
Total Imports	100.0	100.0	100.0	100.0	100.0	100.0	100.0	100.0	100.0
Agricultural Products	24.9	19.4	17.2	10.6	8.1	8.0	8.2	10.3	9.9
Agricultural Requisits	3.0	3.3	2.8	6.5	4.2	6.2	4.1	3.9	3.6
Crude Fertilizers	0.4	0.3	0.4	0.3	1.0	0.1	0.6	0.3	0.2
Manuf Fertilizers	1.5	1.7	2.1	2.5	2.6	3.5	1.8	2.5	3.1
Pesticides	0.4	0.8	0.6	6.6	2.6	0.7	0.8	0.8	1.2
Agric. Machines	0.7	0.5	0.6	3.1	3.0	1.5	0.9	0.3	0.2
Other Imports	72.1	77.3	80.0	82.9	87.7	85.8	87.7	85.8	86.5

Source: FAO Trade Year Book (various issues), U.N., Rome;
IMF Balance of Payments Year Book (various issues), IMF, Washington, D.C.

DISTRIBUTION AND DISPARITIES OF INCOME

Brazilian Economic Expansion and Income Growth

This section will discuss whether there is any positive evidence indicating that the soybean expansion in general, and the high concentration of soybean plantings in specific areas of Brazil in particular, had any implications for the distribution of income both geographically and between sectors of the farming community.

Whereas there is a lack of empirical work directly evaluating any direct connection between soybean plantings and individual incomes, there is evidence available which provides some clues as to the relative position of farmers in the areas where soybeans had their greatest impact compared to farmers elsewhere, and the relative position of soybean producers vis-à-vis other farmers in the same area.

The situation in Brazil is complicated through the traditional existence of the "dual economy," where there is a

Table 7-6   Measures of Inequality for Three Regions of
Brazil, 1970 and 1980, EAP with Positive Incomes
(1980 Cruzeiros)

	TOTAL				
	Mean Income			Gini Coefficient	
Region	1970	1980	% Change	1970	1980
South-Southeast	9746	13925	43	0.545	0.561
North-Northeast	4486	7062	57	0.557	0.586
Center-West	6678	10808	62	0.583	0.583
BRAZIL	8040	11940	49	0.565	0.590

	RURAL				
	Mean Income			Gini Coefficient	
Region	1970	1980	% Change	1970	1980
South-Southeast	4907	8598	75	0.454	0.558
North-Northeast	2681	4145	55	0.404	0.470
Center-West	4569	8459	85	0.339	0.503
BRAZIL	3965	6668	68	0.440	0.544

	URBAN				
	Mean Income			Gini Coefficient	
Region	1970	1980	% Change	1970	1980
South-Southeast	11976	16593	39	0.537	0.532
North-Northeast	7103	9533	34	0.588	0.590
Center-West	9276	13323	44	0.527	0.584
BRAZIL	10778	13912	29	0.552	0.564

Source: Adapted from Denslow, D. and Tyler, W., 1984.

marked contrast between the modern and traditional sectors,
and a marked geographical separation between them. Brazil
was going through a period of substantial economic growth
over the two decades examined here, although there was a
substantial variation in that expansion from year to year, as
demonstrated in Tables 7-1 and 7-2. Indeed, incomes in

Brazil throughout the 1960s and 1970s showed a steady rise (see Table 7-6), with per capita income growing during the decades 1960-1970 and 1970-1980 at annual average rates of 5.0 percent and 4.9 percent respectively (Denslow and Tyler, 1984). However, what is more important in this case are the inter-regional differences, and the differences within the rural sector, rather than the position, however encouraging, across Brazil as a whole. In addition to changes in incomes, the Denslow and Tyler study showed several non-income trends, drawn from the demographic censuses for the years 1960, 1970 and 1980, see Tables 7-7, 7-8 and 7-9, which provide an indirect guide to the relative income position of rural dwellers.

Table 7-7   Non-Income Indications of Well-Being:
Average Literacy Rates By Region - Urban and Rural
1970 & 1980   (Percentages)

Region	Urban		Rural		Total	
	1970	1980	1970	1980	1970	1980
North-Northeast	58.0	65.3	24.0	31.1	39.2	47.7
South-Southeast	79.0	83.4	54.0	65.1	71.1	79.3
Center-West	71.0	74.1	37.0	48.3	55.9	63.3
BRAZIL	73.0	78.3	40.0	47.9	59.4	68.7

Source: Denslow and Tyler, 1984.

Table 7-8   School Enrollment Rates, 1970 and 1980
(Percentages)

Region	Grades 1-8		Grades 9 - 12	
	1970	1980	1970	1980
North-Northeast	62.0	74.0	6.0	17.0
South-Southeast	90.0	99.0	12.0	26.0
Center-West	77.0	93.0	7.0	21.0
BRAZIL	80.0	90.0	10.0	23.0

Source: Denslow and Tyler, 1984.

Table 7-9   Non-Income Indications of Well-Being:
                   Piped Water Supply and Sewerage Services by Region, 1970 and 1980

| | Piped Water Supply | | | Sewerage - Piped or Septic Tank | | |
| | % Households | | | % Households | | |
Region	1970	1980	% Change[1]	1970	1980	% Change[1]
North - Northeast	12.4	30.1	13.1	8.0	16.4	11.2
Urban	28.7	57.9	12.7	18.6	30.9	10.8
Rural	0.5	2.6	19.6	0.3	2.0	22.1
South-Southeast	44.2	65.9	8.4	37.2	56.2	8.5
Urban	63.3	82.6	8.6	53.4	68.3	8.4
Rural	3.5	3.9	1.6	3.6	11.5	12.1
Center-West	19.6	38.2	13.6	12.6	18.3	11.0
Urban	39.9	61.9	13.5	25.7	30.1	10.7
Rural	1.6	2.8	10.0	0.9	3.1	16.8
BRAZIL	32.2	53.2	9.3	26.6	41.5	8.9
Urban	54.4	75.8	9.4	44.2	57.4	8.7
Rural	2.6	3.2	4.1	2.0	6.2	13.3

[1] Annual compunded rates for the number of households covered.

Source: Denslow and Tyler, 1984.

substantial variation in that expansion from year to year, as
demonstrated in Tables 7-1 and 7-2. Indeed, incomes in
Brazil throughout the 1960s and 1970s showed a steady rise,
(see Table 7-6), with per capita income growing during the
decades 1960-1970 and 1970-1981 at annual average rates of
5.0 percent and 4.9 percent respectively (Denslow and Tyler,
1984). However, what is more important in this case are the
inter-regional differences, and the differences within the
rural sector, rather than the position, however encouraging,
across Brazil as a whole. In addition to changes in incomes,
the Denslow and Tyler study showed several non-income trends,
drawn from the demographic censuses for the years 1960, 1970
and 1980, see Tables 7-7, 7-8 and 7-9, which provide an
indirect guide to the relative income position of rural
dwellers.

Regional imbalances

The 1980 demographic census indicated that the apparent stability in income distribution disguises significant differentials within sectors. Two major changes during the 1970s tend to offset each other. First, the differences between average incomes among sectors narrowed, thus reducing inequality, whereas on the other hand, inequality within the agricultural sector dramatically increased as shown in Table 7-6 (Denslow and Tyler, 1984). Table 7-6, also shows that regional disparities as a whole diminished in the 1970s, with average income rising more rapidly in the Northeast than in the more prosperous Southeast. However, when these numbers

Table 7-10   Government Expenditures and Annual Flow of Subsidized Credit:
                              Brazil, 1970-77

(Millions of Current Cruzeiros)

Year	Government Expenditures			Rural Loans from Banco do Brasil & Comm. Banks	Other subsidized loans			Ratio of loans to government expenditures
	Current	Capital	Total		Federal Banks	State Banks	Total loans	
1970	20,512	8,273	28,785	2,676	1,262	250	4,188	0.15
1971	26,779	10,596	37,375	3,519	819	492	4,830	0.13
1972	34,688	13,854	48,542	5,985	2,466	1,199	9,650	0.20
1973	46,190	18,061	64,251	13,606	3,907	1,837	19,350	0.30
1974	65,455	28,715	94,170	18,749	12,876	4,023	35,648	0.38
1975	99,345	43,359	142,704	36,211	23,484	6,275	65,970	0.46
1976	157,434	65,643	223,077	42,717	41,423	13,949	98,089	0.44
1977	220,840	90,487	311,327	53,240	58,902	18,584	130,726	0.42

Source: Adapted from Sayad (1979).

are disaggregated into sectoral differences, then increases in rural incomes were far greater in the Southeast than in the Northeast. Although inequality among sectors fell, inequalities within agriculture appear to have increased.

There are several possible explanations for the increases in inequality within agriculture. First, in addition to lifting agricultural incomes in Brazil in general, the surging production of specific export crops such as soybeans may provide part of the answer. Second, perhaps the most important explanation may lie in the growth and the distribution of subsidized credit during the decade of the 1970s

(Homem de Melo, 1978, Sayad, 1979). The massive supply of subsidized credit was the pivot of Brazilian agricultural policy. More significantly, its distribution between regions, farms, and crops, is likely to have been a fundamental reason for much of the substantial differences within agriculture of income growth and general well-being over the period in question. The vital part soybeans played in the expansion of agriculture and the supply of heavily subsidized credit to encourage this expansion, together with the limited regional participation of soybeans in terms of area in Brazil, provides—if only by way of circumstantial evidence—a very strong indication of the significance of the explosive growth of the soybean crop on the pattern of income distribution in Brazil.

Indeed, it may be construed that the greater the resource diversion toward a single sector within the rural economy, the greater will be the growth in income where that sector is situated. Conversely, the lack of resource diversion to less favored areas or less favored enterprises such as the Northeast or the production of domestic crops (upon which the lower income groups are so heavily dependent), will result in a relative decline in income in the area where the potential for production of the favored crop does not exist. The relative poverty of the Northeast compared to the prosperous Southeast is displayed in other evidence in addition to income, such as calorific intake, provision of the basic necessities of life such as piped water and electricity, amount of schooling, possession of consumer durables, and so on. On all counts there has been improvement, but the growth has indeed been greater in the Southeast than the Northeast.

The resource which was diverted with the greatest effect was rural credit. The enormous inflow of credit into agriculture as a result of successive government policy initiatives over the period had a considerable effect upon the sector. The National System of Rural Credit, created in 1965, was comprised of the Banco do Brasil and the commercial banks. The Banco do Brasil, which is state-owned, holds 40 percent of the nation's demand deposits, and puts into effect many of the government's policy decisions (Sayad, 1979). The government mandates the percentage of demand deposits to be lent to the rural sector and the level of interest rates on the loans. Initially the interest rates were fixed at 17 percent, and were later lowered to 15 percent at a time when inflation was running at between 20 and 40 percent.

After 1973, Brazilian economic trends shifted dramatically. Oil price rises and the deteriorating balance of payments led to lower growth rates, and both inflation and interest rates soared. The rural credit system was maintained at a 15 percent nominal interest rate, with several special lending programs at even lower rates. The net result was the diversion of a huge proportion of Brazil's total lending into agriculture at a very high level of subsidy. Table 7-10 shows the annual flows of subsidized credit (rural and other types) over the period 1970-1977, and their ratio to total government spending. Rural loans were the most significant in terms of subsidy. In the latter years of the period, the total value of subsidized loans represented over 45 percent of all government expenditures.

In the same years, the total value of rural loans was equal to as much as 90 percent of farm income in Brazil (Sayad, 1979). Table 3-7 shows the extent of the credit subsidy in 1980 cruzeiros. In 1976 the level of total agricultural credit rose as high as 94 percent of total agricultural GDP, with the subsidy element representing virtually 18 percent.

One of the greatest attractions of using subsidized rural loans as agricultural incentives was the simplicity of operation. Sayad states that "planners seemed to believe that rural credit programs could work magic and change the private sector pattern of investment quickly, without inflationary pressures or uncertainties." It was far easier to implement planning decisions through credit, rather than having to alter tax laws or obtain approval from the legislative body for additional expenditures; the whole program could be contained within the centralized bureaucracy of the Banco do Brasil (Sayad, 1979). Under these circumstances, the very nature of banking. and the natural prudence of bankers would appear to shift the advantage toward borrowers who offered the better collateral and least risk, and were most liquid. These tended to be the larger farmers, who were in more favored areas and who produced crops with the most attractive returns.

Table 7-11 shows the division of all farms and farmland according to region. This in itself is an indication of the geographic distribution of wealth, 47 percent of the farms are in the Northeast with 24 percent of the land, and 17 percent are in the Southeast. However, in the regional breakdown of total loan contracts and their respective values under the Rural Credit Scheme (see Table 7-12), the distribution is quite different. Only 15 percent of loans went to the Northeast with a value of 13 percent of the total, whereas 38.7 percent went to the Southeast and 38.1 percent

Table 7-11   Geographical Distribution of Farms and
               Land in Farms: Brazil, 1980

Region	Number of Farms	%	Area	%
North	408,173	7.9	41,559,420	11.4
Northeast	2,447,513	47.4	88,443,907	24.2
Southeast	890,869	17.3	73,502,906	20.1
South	1,145,548	22.2	47,911,723	13.1
Center-West	267,748	5.2	113,436,463	31.1
BRAZIL	5,159,851	100.0	364,854,419	100.0

Source: Censo Agropecuario 1980, IBGE, Rio de Janeiro.

Table 7-12   Distribution of Rural Credit According to
               Region: Brazil, 1978

Region	Number of Contracts	%	Value of Contracts (Cr$ 000)	%
North	34,383	1.8	5,376,217	2.3
Northeast	290,876	15.3	30,584,827	13.1
Southeast	733,215	38.7	86,293,330	36.9
South	721,743	38.1	88,338,176	37.8
Center-West	115,306	6.1	23,349,904	10.0
BRAZIL	1,895,523	100.0	233,942,454	100.0

Source: Quintana, 1982.

to the South, representing 36.9 and 37.8 percent of the total
value respectively.   The   substantial subsidy element within
the Rural Credit loans therefore provided a significant
income advantage to farmers in the Southeast and Southern
regions.

8
Foreign Trade Aspects

WORLD MARKET SHARES

The history of Brazil's involvement in domestic soybean production has been set out in some detail in the previous chapters. How did Brazil stand in the world production league during these years? In terms of world shares in soybean production, the main participants are listed in Table 8-1. The growth of world soybean production after 1960, including the Brazilian participation, is displayed in Figure 8-1. From annual figures produced by The Food and Agriculture Organization of the United Nations (FAO) it can be ascertained that the growth of the soybean crop worldwide escalated from 30 million tons to over 93.5 million during the period 1960 through 1982, an increase of more than three fold, representing an annual growth rate of some 5.5 percent. Brazil started at less than 1 percent of total world production at the beginning of the period, and increased its share to over 15 percent of the total by 1982.

As for the world market in soybean and soybean products, from the time Brazil made its entry in 1964 to the end of the period examined, world exports of whole beans grew from 6.3 million to 29.3 million tons, world exports of soybean meal from 2.3 million to 20.7 million tons, and soybean oil from .7 million to 3.5 million tons. The breakdown of this growth between the major participants over the period is shown in Table 8-2. Brazil's impact was very substantial particularly, as one might expect, in the pro-

Figure 8-1

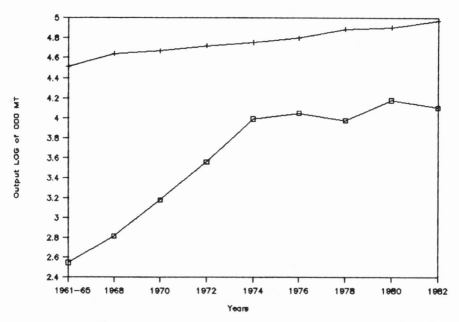

World Production and Brazil's Share

cessed product market, increasing its share of world soybean
meal exports from 2 percent in 1964 to as high as 40 percent
by 1982. Brazil did not enter the world soybean oil market
until the early 1970s. In 1972 it provided only 5 percent of
the soybean oil traded; within four years it had achieved a
participation of over 25 percent, a share which Brazil
virtually maintained in 1982. In both meal and oil Brazil
was to seriously erode the U.S. dominance in the world
market.

Table 8-3 represents the total value of the world
soybean and soybean products market over the period. During
the latter 1970s, virtually one quarter of the world's
soybean trade, in terms of dollar value, was represented by
Brazil. The extent to which this impacted upon the U.S.
share is suggested by Table 8-4. It is interesting to
examine this as trade as soybean equivalents. In soybean
equivalents, by 1976 Brazil had nearly 19 percent of the
world market, and by the end of the decade its share exceeded

Table 8-1   World Production of Soybeans, 1948-82
(000 Metric Tons)

Country	1948-52	1961-65	1968	1970	1972	1974	1976	1978	1980	1982
United States	7312	19560	30023	30910	34581	33569	35042	50859	48920	59610
Brazil	78	353	654	1508	3666	9876	11227	9535	15156	12810
Argentina	0	12	22	27	78	496	695	3700	4150	4150
Paraguay	0	8	14	22	97	170	173	549	600	690
China (mainland)	7282	10540	10670	11500	11240	11860	12453	7565	7940	9030
Other	1280	1995	2383	2554	2678	832	3435	5156	4644	7270
World Total	15952	32468	43766	46521	52340	56803	63025	77364	80910	93560

(Percentage of Total)

Country	1948-52	1961-6	1968	1970	1972	1974	1976	1978	1980	1982
United States	45.8	60.2	68.6	66.4	66.1	59.1	55.6	65.7	60.5	63.7
Brazil	0.5	1.1	1.5	3.2	7.0	17.4	17.8	12.3	18.7	13.7
Argentina	0.0	0.0	0.1	0.1	0.1	0.9	1.1	4.8	4.5	4.4
Paraguay	0.0	0.0	0.0	0.0	0.2	0.3	0.3	0.7	0.7	0.7
China (mainland)	45.6	32.5	24.4	24.7	21.5	20.9	19.8	9.8	9.8	9.7
Other	8.0	6.1	5.4	5.5	5.1	1.5	5.5	6.7	5.7	7.8
World Total	100	100	100	100	100	100	100	100	100	100

Source: FAO Production Year Book (various issues);
USDA/FAS--Oil Seeds and Products (various issues).

Table 8-2   Soybeans and Products: World Market Shares 1964-82,
Exports   (000 Metric Tons)

Soybeans

	1964	%	1968	%	1972	%	1976	%	1980	%	1982	%
U.S.A	5702	91	8012	92	11993	87	15332	78	21786	81	25280	86
Brazil	0	0	66	1	213	2	78	0	1549	6	860	3
Argentina	0	0	0	0	0	0	78	0	2709	10	1880	6
Others	588	9	678	8	1569	11	4264	22	843	3	1300	4
World Total	6290	100	8756	100	13776	100	19753	100	26888	100	29320	100

Soybean Meal

	1964	%	1968	%	1972	%	1976	%	1980	%	1982	%
U.S.A	1568	68	2698	72	3619	55	4862	43	7024	39	6270	30
Brazil	44	2	235	6	1405	21	4374	39	6582	37	8350	40
Argentina	0	0	0	0	0	0	176	2	440	2	740	4
Others	697	30	793	21	1522	23	1936	17	3869	22	5380	26
World Total	2309	100	3726	100	6546	100	11348	100	17916	100	20740	100

Soybean Oil

	1964	%	1968	%	1972	%	1976	%	1980	%	1982	%
U.S.A	578	80	427	72	587	53	507	28	1220	37	940	27
Brazil	0	0	0	0	60	5	498	27	523	16	850	24
Argentina	0	0	0	0	0	0	64	4	106	3	120	3
Others	144	20	169	28	459	41	758	42	1410	43	1590	45
World Total	721	100	595	100	1105	100	1827	100	3259	100	3500	100

Source: USDA/FAS; FAO.

Table 8-3   World Market and Brazil's Share of Soybeans and Soybean Products
             as Total Value of Exports in (Million $U.S), 1964-80

Year	Soybeans (World)	Meal	Oil	Total	Soybean (Brazil)	Meal	Oil	Total	Brazil(%)
1964	637.49	203.72	175.24	1016.45	0.00	3.02	0.00	3.02	0.30
1965	748.74	247.46	202.74	1198.95	7.35	7.68	0.00	15.02	1.25
1966	860.48	297.32	160.21	1318.01	13.03	14.59	0.00	27.62	2.10
1967	884.39	324.42	182.37	1391.19	29.24	10.22	0.00	39.46	2.84
1968	900.25	350.95	131.25	1382.44	6.29	18.93	0.00	25.22	1.82
1969	914.30	387.24	150.50	1452.05	29.25	23.41	0.00	52.66	3.63
1970	1300.99	505.58	311.52	2118.09	27.08	43.64	0.77	71.49	3.38
1971	1415.40	610.70	407.89	2433.99	24.31	81.53	2.25	108.09	4.44
1972	1730.97	744.19	318.61	2793.76	127.93	152.35	14.70	294.97	10.56
1973	3360.08	1839.11	374.04	5573.22	494.15	422.63	33.20	949.99	17.05
1975	3699.92	1462.30	946.85	6109.06	684.90	465.77	153.59	1304.26	21.35
1976	4252.44	2079.01	830.87	7162.32	788.54	795.00	196.42	1779.97	24.85
1977	5467.41	2666.62	1209.18	9343.21	709.65	1145.71	255.92	2111.27	22.60
1978	6004.62	3014.16	1610.02	10628.80	169.89	1049.00	294.91	1513.80	14.24
1979	6864.95	3470.32	1998.23	12333.50	179.51	1138.01	333.91	1651.42	13.39
1980	7133.39	4219.73	2000.93	13354.05	393.93	1449.01	421.25	2264.19	16.96

Source: FAO Trade Year Book (various issues), FAO, Rome.

Table 8-4   Soybeans and Products: World Market Shares in
                Soybean Equivalents[1], 1960-82
                Exports   (000 Metric Tons)

	1964	%	1968	%	1972	%	1976	%	1980	%	1982	%
U.S.A	10810	82	13818	82	19857	70	24417	55	37476	55	38501	51
Brazil	58	0	375	2	2384	8	8469	19	12988	19	16353	22
Argentina	0	0	0	0	0	0	648	1	3848	6	3488	5
Others	2263	17	2612	16	5990	21	10808	24	13367	20	16765	22
World	13131	100	16805	100	28232	100	44342	100	67679	100	75107	100

[1]Calculated as Soybeans + 1/.19(Soybean Meal) + 1/.76(Soybean Oil).
Source: USDA/FAS, FAO.

20 percent. World trade in soybean equivalents grew by an annual rate of nearly 10 percent for the whole of the twenty-year period, with Brazil's trade increasing by an annual rate of over 19 percent over the second ten years.

This demonstrates that Brazil's soybean exports did have a substantial impact on world soybean trade both in terms of volume and value. At a time when world production and trade were growing very substantially, Brazil was able to capitalize on the opportunity and carve out a substantial share of the market.

Table 8-5   Share of Soybeans as a percentage of Total
             Exports and Agricultural Product Exports, 1960-82

Year	Soybean Exports as a Percentage of Total Exports	Soybean Exports as a Percentage of Agricultural Product Exports
1960	0.0	–
1961	0.5	–
1962	0.7	–
1963	0.5	–
1964	0.2	0.3
1965	0.9	1.2
1966	1.6	2.0
1967	2.4	2.9
1968	1.3	1.6
1969	2.3	2.7
1970	2.6	3.3
1971	3.7	5.0
1972	7.4	9.3
1973	15.3	19.5
1974	11.2	15.5
1975	15.0	22.2
1976	17.6	25.3
1977	17.7	24.8
1978	12.0	18.8
1979	10.8	18.1
1980	11.2	24.2
1981	13.0	32.8
1982	10.5	

Source: FAO Trade Year Book--FAO, Rome;
        International Financial Statistics--IMF, Washington D.C.

Table 8-6   Brazil: Domestic and Export Market Shares of Total Soybean Production, 1960-82
Relative Shares (000 metric Tons & Percentages)[1]

Year	Total Soybeans			Other*	Crush	%	Production		Domestic Market				Export Market			
	Output	Export	%				Meal	Oil	Meal	%	Oil	%	Meal	%	Oil	%
1960	206	0	0.0	74	132	64.1	98	22	98	100.0	22	100.0	0	0.0	0	0.0
1961	271	73	26.9	55	143	52.8	106	24	106	100.0	26	108.3	0	0.0	0	0.0
1962	345	97	28.1	75	173	50.1	129	30	129	100.0	33	110.0	0	0.0	0	0.0
1963	323	34	10.5	89	200	61.9	150	35	88	58.7	36	102.9	62	41.3	0	0.0
1964	305	0	0.0	75	227	74.4	172	40	128	74.4	42	105.0	44	25.6	0	0.0
1965	523	75	14.3	149	289	55.3	224	52	119	53.1	61	117.3	105	46.9	0	0.0
1966	595	121	20.3	64	404	67.9	307	71	123	40.1	82	115.5	185	60.3	0	0.0
1967	716	305	42.6	74	335	46.8	254	62	140	55.1	77	124.2	125	49.2	0	0.0
1968	654	66	10.1	88	493	75.4	377	89	139	36.9	89	100.0	235	62.3	0	0.0
1969	1057	310	29.3	105	630	59.6	465	110	105	22.6	113	102.7	295	63.4	0	0.0
1970	1508	290	19.2	150	1025	68.0	794	189	173	21.8	194	102.6	525	66.1	1	0.5
1971	2077	296	14.3	200	1600	77.0	1224	295	251	20.5	282	95.6	905	73.9	13	4.4
1972	3223	1024	31.8	331	2326	72.2	1803	440	248	13.8	372	84.5	1405	77.9	68	15.5
1973	5012	1788	35.7	474	2651	52.9	2014	496	603	29.9	397	80.0	1582	78.6	82	16.5
1974	7876	2863	36.4	685	4267	54.2	3245	807	718	22.1	694	86.0	2407	74.2	16	2.0
1975	9893	3516	35.5	880	5279	53.4	4038	1020	840	20.8	682	66.9	3134	77.6	321	31.5
1976	11223	3352	29.9	925	6781	60.4	5157	1191	970	18.8	850	71.4	4374	84.8	430	36.1
1977	12513	2581	20.6	1090	8661	69.2	6616	1585	1438	21.7	1025	64.7	5328	80.5	560	35.3
1978	9541	659	6.9	838	8882	93.1	6842	1629	1461	21.4	1110	68.1	5419	79.2	522	32.0
1979	10240	638	6.2	895	9094	88.8	7040	1669	1971	28.0	1309	78.4	5176	73.5	459	27.5
1980	15156	1533	10.1	920	13009	85.8	9968	2463	2595	26.1	1516	61.6	6582	66.0	809	32.8
1981	15200	1502	9.9	890	13796	90.8	10067	2585	2271	22.6	1490	57.6	8891	88.3	1212	46.9
1982	12835	797	6.2	895	12728	99.2	9879	2392	1956	19.8	1505	62.9	7957	80.5	873	36.5

[1] Percentages might exceed 100 because of imports
Source: FAO Trade Year Book (various issues);
USDA Foreign Agriculture Service—Oil Seeds and Products (various issues).

How important was this for Brazil? It was intimated in Chapter 3 that Brazil's policy makers, while discouraging exports in the 1950s and early 1960s, began to give cautious support for expansion starting in the middle of the 1960s. But it was not until ten years later, in response to substantial increases in world market--buoyed by the embargo introduced by the United States on its export of soybeans-- that soybean exports were heavily encouraged and the period of rapid expansion began. It is interesting to note the conclusions of Williams and Thompson in this context, inasmuch as their findings showed that given the Brazilian agricultural policy structure, without undue interference with exports, the Brazilian contribution to world trade in soybeans could have been in fact even higher. Using a mathematical model of the world soybean market, they concluded that the explosion in Brazilian soybean production in the 1960s was in fact generated by world price, but that during the next decade, Brazilian government policies led to lower domestic soybean prices and hence to a slower rate of growth than would otherwise have occurred. The net effect of this was lower Brazilian supplies, lower exports of soybean products and, as Brazil's market share by this time had a direct influence on world prices, consequently higher prices for whole soybeans and for soybean products. This led to lower world trade in soybeans than otherwise might have been the case, but to higher exports from the United States (Williams and Thompson, 1984b).

The importance of soybeans and soybean products to Brazilian foreign earnings, as a percentage both of total exports and of total agricultural exports is shown in Table 8-5. It can be seen that for much of the 1970s the shares were in the order of 17.5 and 20 percent respectively. The shares of the domestic and export markets of total Brazilian production of soybeans and soybean products appears in Table 8-6. Brazil, while maintaining domestic supplies of soybean oil, in the early years kept oil exports at a minimal level. However, around 80 percent of all soybean meal produced by the crushing industry was exported, and by the mid-1970s oil exports themselves had reached over 35 percent of total output. As suggested earlier, one of the major factors behind the growing demand for soymeal as a high protein supplement to livestock feed came from the modernization and rapid expansion of Brazil's own domestic poultry industry.

WORLD DEMAND

The rapid growth of the world soybean trade in the 1960s and 1970s followed a trend that commenced immediately after World War II, representing a substantial worldwide expansion in the demand for fats, oils, and high-protein meals, stimulated by rising population and income in many countries (Houck, Ryan and Subotnik, 1972). The relationships between the various components of this category are complex, as there is a considerable degree of substitution possible between the constituents. Utimately, however, the demand for one commodity rather than another is dependent on price. In addition, the overall trend masks substantial disparities in consumption among and within different regions of the world.

Oilseeds are a major source of much of the world's leading food oils. Production of oilseeds for the international market largely originated in European colonies. Originally production was organized for internal needs, however, as former colonies gained independence, oilseed production was maintained to meet both domestic and foreign demand. In addition, the production of oilseeds as a cash crop for export became very attractive to a number of developing countries as a means of earning foreign exchange (Houck, Ryan and Subotnik, 1972).

The contribution of soybeans to world trade was negligible before 1950. Exports from the U.S., the world's dominant supplier until the emergence of Brazil, did not exceed 300,000 tons until 1949. From then on, expansion was rapid. As can be seen from Table 8-7, the overall demand for all soybean products more than doubled between 1962 and 1972, and then doubled again by the end of the next decade. Part of this growth was in the increasing world demand for oils and oil meals, but much was due to the relative competitiveness of soybeans in relation to the more traditional sources. Soybeans now have a major place in the world oil and meal markets.

Table 8-7 shows that the dominant importing region, in both whole beans and soybean meal, has been Western Europe, which has taken up over half these commodities traded on the world market. However, when one examines each regional market (see Table 8-8), there is growth indicative of rising demand for fats and oils in other regions, notably Eastern Europe and the USSR, but also Asia.

The demand in Europe for oil meals has close political links with the creation of the European Economic Community (EEC) and the Common Agricultural Policy (CAP) which followed. One of the main goals of the CAP was the drive for

Table 8-7　　　　World Market For Soybeans And Soybean Products: Imports
(Million Metric Tons)

Soybeans

	1964	%	1968	%	1972	%	1976	%	1980	%	1982	%
EEC-9 (Net)[1]	3183.22	51.9	3620.09	43.3	6494.92	46.9	9014.54	45.6	11702.83	42.5	11895.96	42.1
Rest of Europe	299.80	4.9	1186.39	14.2	2008.90	14.5	3048.38	15.4	5315.70	19.3	4962.05	17.6
USSR	0.00	0.0	0.00	0.0	296.80	2.1	1570.64	7.9	1085.12	3.9	1506.10	5.3
Africa	0.00	0.0	0.00	0.0	4.86	0.0	18.60	0.1	40.40	0.1	95.71	0.3
N'th & Cent. Am.	525.14	8.6	331.24	4.0	340.97	2.5	815.45	4.1	1491.04	5.4	1091.25	3.9
South America	24.80	0.4	47.75	0.6	102.23	0.7	43.32	0.2	504.68	1.8	1437.35	5.1
Asia & Oceania	2095.97	34.2	3179.14	38.0	4598.85	33.2	5272.83	26.7	7393.27	26.9	7239.46	25.6
World Total	6128.93	100.0	8364.61	100.0	13847.52	100.0	19783.76	100.0	27533.05	100.0	28227.88	100.0

Soybean Meal

	1964	%	1968	%	1972	%	1976	%	1980	%	1982	%
EEC-9 (Net)[1]	1007.29	50.0	1982.78	60.3	3201.15	43.6	3892.38	35.4	6246.16	35.2	7499.35	36.6
Rest of Europe	732.70	36.4	1005.89	30.6	3645.02	49.6	5972.84	54.3	8282.31	46.7	8308.64	40.5
USSR	0.00	0.0	0.00	0.0	0.00	0.0	0.00	0.0	345.90	1.9	1374.00	6.7
Africa	0.45	0.0	2.26	0.1	6.50	0.1	21.76	0.2	157.04	0.9	314.27	1.5
North & Cent. Am	240.72	11.9	250.29	7.6	316.76	4.3	473.91	4.3	877.68	4.9	763.24	3.7
South America	7.37	0.4	0.00	0.0	23.09	0.3	165.72	1.5	364.54	2.1	604.50	2.9
Asia & Oceania	25.93	1.3	45.70	1.4	153.49	2.1	479.07	4.4	1478.79	8.3	1644.65	8.0
World Total	2014.46	100.0	3286.92	100.0	7346.01	100.0	11005.67	100.0	17752.42	100.0	20508.65	100.0

Soybean Oil

	1964	%	1968	%	1972	%	1976	%	1980	%	1982	%
EEC-9 (Net)[1]	-5.29	-0.8	-51.53	-11.5	-157.25	-17.5	53.04	3.3	-215.22	-7.6	-305.58	-10.1
Rest of Europe	291.18	42.3	69.39	15.5	297.37	33.1	520.50	32.3	560.07	19.9	495.53	16.4
USSR	0.00	0.0	0.00	0.0	86.66	9.7	0.00	0.0	52.39	1.9	99.08	3.3
Africa	62.42	9.1	95.98	21.5	119.90	13.4	150.96	9.4	370.89	13.2	554.69	18.4
North & Cent. Am	31.07	4.5	49.49	11.1	56.07	6.2	98.20	6.1	165.60	5.9	213.64	7.1
South America	48.68	7.1	46.95	10.5	62.60	7.0	185.22	11.5	288.65	10.3	382.54	12.7
Asia & Oceania	260.50	37.8	236.61	52.9	432.18	48.2	602.50	37.4	1592.67	56.6	1578.99	52.3
World Total	688.56	100.0	446.89	100.0	897.53	100.0	1610.43	100.0	2815.06	100.0	3018.88	100.0

[1] Imports gross unless otherwise stated; EEC-9 shown net as exports represent to a large extent inter-European trade.
Source: FAO Trade Year Book (Various Issues); USDA Foreign Agriculture Service—Oil Seeds and Products (Various Issues).

Table 8-8   Growth in World Demand for Soybean Products, 1964-82
Imports (Million Metric Tons)

Soybeans

	1964	%	1968	%	1972	%	1976	%	1980	%	1982	%
EEC-9 (Net)[1]	3183.22	51.9	3620.09	43.3	6494.92	46.9	9014.54	45.6	11702.83	42.5	11895.96	42.1
Rest of Europe	299.80	4.9	1186.39	14.2	2008.90	14.5	3048.38	15.4	5315.70	19.3	4962.05	17.6
USSR	0.00	0.0	0.00	0.0	296.80	2.1	1570.64	7.9	1085.12	3.9	1506.10	5.3
Africa	0.00	0.0	0.00	0.0	4.86	0.0	18.60	0.1	40.40	0.1	95.71	0.3
N'th & Cent. Am.	525.14	8.6	331.24	4.0	340.97	2.5	815.45	4.1	1491.04	5.4	1091.25	3.9
South America	24.80	0.4	47.75	0.6	102.23	0.7	43.32	0.2	504.68	1.8	1437.35	5.1
Asia & Oceania	2095.97	34.2	3179.14	38.0	4598.85	33.2	5272.83	26.7	7393.27	26.9	7239.46	25.6
World Total	6128.93	100.0	8364.61	100.0	13847.52	100.0	19783.76	100.0	27533.05	100.0	28227.88	100.0

Soybean Meal

	1964	%	1968	%	1972	%	1976	%	1980	%	1982	%
EEC-9 (Net)[1]	1007.29	50.0	1982.78	60.3	3201.15	43.6	3892.38	35.4	6246.16	35.2	7499.35	36.6
Rest of Europe	732.70	36.4	1005.89	30.6	3645.02	49.6	5972.84	54.3	8282.31	46.7	8308.64	40.5
USSR	0.00	0.0	0.00	0.0	0.00	0.0	0.00	0.0	345.90	1.9	1374.00	6.7
Africa	0.45	0.0	2.26	0.1	6.50	0.1	21.76	0.2	157.04	0.9	314.27	1.5
North & Cent. Am	240.72	11.9	250.29	7.6	316.76	4.3	473.91	4.3	877.68	4.9	763.24	3.7
South America	7.37	0.4	0.00	0.0	23.09	0.3	165.72	1.5	364.54	2.1	604.50	2.9
Asia & Oceania	25.93	1.3	45.70	1.4	153.49	2.1	479.07	4.4	1478.79	8.3	1644.65	8.0
World Total	2014.46	100.0	3286.92	100.0	7346.01	100.0	11005.67	100.0	17752.42	100.0	20508.65	100.0

Soybean Oil

	1964	%	1968	%	1972	%	1976	%	1980	%	1982	%
EEC-9 (Net)[1]	-5.29	-0.8	-51.53	-11.5	-157.25	-17.5	53.04	3.3	-216.22	-7.6	-305.58	-10.1
Rest of Europe	291.18	42.3	69.39	15.5	297.37	33.1	520.50	32.3	560.07	19.9	495.53	16.4
USSR	0.00	0.0	0.00	0.0	86.66	9.7	0.00	0.0	52.39	1.9	99.08	3.3
Africa	62.42	9.1	95.98	21.5	119.90	13.4	150.96	9.4	370.89	13.2	554.69	18.4
North & Cent. Am.	31.07	4.5	49.49	11.1	56.07	6.2	98.20	6.1	165.60	5.9	213.64	7.1
South America	48.68	7.1	46.95	10.5	62.60	7.0	185.22	11.5	288.65	10.3	382.54	12.7
Asia & Oceania	260.50	37.8	236.61	52.9	432.18	48.2	602.50	37.4	1592.67	56.6	1578.99	52.3
World Total	688.56	100.0	446.89	100.0	897.53	100.0	1610.43	100.0	2815.06	100.0	3018.88	100.0

[1] Imports gross unless otherwise stated; EEC-9 shown net as exports represent to a large extent inter-European trade.
Source: FAO Trade Year Book (various issues); USDA FAS--Oil Seeds and Products (various issues).

self-sufficiency within the community. This was rapidly reflected in a mushrooming livestock sector which created a substantial demand for soybean meal. In the EEC the price relationship between soybeans and feed grains is much closer to that in the United States, therefore the growth in the livestock sector had particular relevance to the use of soybean meal. The main reason for this being the structure of the CAP which allows soybeans into Europe tariff free, whereas feed grains are subject to the EEC tariff barriers.

DESTINATION OF EXPORTS

Where are Brazil's main markets for its soybeans and soybean products? Tables 8-9, 8-10, and 8-11 show the distribution of Brazilian exports according to country of destination, both in quantities and in total value. As described earlier, in developing its domestic crushing capacity, Brazil has only been involved with limited exports of whole beans. Only a few countries imported Brazilian soybeans. During the first years of the period the EEC (then consisting of 9 members) represented the largest market region. As Brazilian exports of whole beans mushroomed in the early 1970s the EEC absorbed most of the tonnage. However, from the mid 1970s, as Brazil's processing capacity expanded and whole bean exports were constrained, the EEC's share fell with Spain and the USSR becoming major purchasers.

Soybean meal exports were of much greater significance, and the distribution of importing nations far wider. The EEC was by far the most significant market for Brazil but, as Table 8-10 shows, Brazil exported soybean meal to many other parts of the world. Of note was the increasing importance to Brazil of the Eastern Bloc nations after 1975, particularly East Germany, Hungary, and Yugoslavia. In Asia, Brazil developed important outlets in the Philippines and Thailand, with Japan also taking some tonnage. In the latter part of the period, new markets evolved in Africa and the Middle East. Brazil had virtually no exports of soybean oil until the latter half of the 1970s; Europe, being self-sufficient,

Table 8-9

Soybean exports from Brazil by Destination, 1965-82

Destination	1965		1968		1970		1975		1980		1982	
	Quant. (000 MT)	Value US$M	Quant. (000 MT)	Value US$M	Quant. (000 MT)	Value US$M	Quant. (000 MT)	Value US$M	Quant. (000 MT)	Value US$M	Quant. (000 MT)	Value US$M
Europe(EEC-9)	67.72	6.63	47.66	4.48	192.66	17.94	2121.00	438.79	573.93	140.00	18.49	4.48
Spain	6.30	0.60	4.65	0.46	38.58	3.60	605.78	124.16	705.65	180.18	27.04	6.57
Bulgaria	-	-	10.00	1.02	16.86	1.60	-	-	-	-	-	-
Germany (DR)	-	-	2.92	0.28	41.24	3.92	-	-	-	-	-	-
USSR	-	-	-	-	-	-	438.21	86.73	118.34	33.37	255.48	63.14
Japan	-	-	-	-	-	-	43.76	9.35	39.52	10.57	-	-
Malaysia	1.26	0.12	-	-	-	-	-	-	-	-	12.60	3.18
China	-	-	-	-	-	-	31.51	6.71	-	-	-	-
Mexico	-	-	-	-	-	-	-	-	42.00	12.05	178.05	42.10
Others	-	-	0.64	0.06	0.28	0.03	92.75	19.17	69.56	17.77	9.15	3.99
Total Exports	75.29	7.34	65.86	6.29	289.62	27.08	3333.00	684.90	1549.00	393.93	500.80	123.46

Source: Commodity Statistics, United Nations, N.Y. (various issues).

126

Table 8-10

Soybean Meal Exports from Brazil by Destination

Destination	1965 Quant. (000 MT)	1965 Value US$M	1968 Quant. (000 MT)	1968 Value US$M	1970 Quant. (000 MT)	1970 Value US$M	1975 Quant. (000 MT)	1975 Value US$M	1980 Quant. (000 MT)	1980 Value US$M	1982 Quant. (000 MT)	1982 Value US$M
Europe(EEC-9)	273.95	18.33	213.13	17.14	791.11	59.25	1880.00	270.28	4621.00	1000.59	4695.00	961.30
Spain	0.30	0.02	-	-	-	-	141.83	20.75	53.21	9.65	55.96	10.54
Portugal	-	-	1.11	0.09	30.12	2.60	68.32	12.28	108.09	23.01	-	-
Germany (DR)	-	-	-	-	6.15	0.53	8.50	1.00	20.00	4.07	401.83	84.85
Bulgaria	-	-	-	-	-	-	136.40	20.02	-	-	53.18	10.58
Czechoslovakia	-	-	-	-	-	-	118.31	18.16	135.07	31.46	196.19	38.01
Hungary	-	-	2.00	0.17	46.43	3.79	116.13	18.50	212.30	47.77	376.41	83.53
Poland	-	-	-	-	2.59	0.22	320.46	47.35	806.22	175.25	291.13	61.20
Romania	-	-	-	-	6.97	0.59	167.58	25.09	-	-	15.30	2.85
Yugoslavia	-	-	-	-	-	-	152.10	23.74	159.21	42.29	34.04	6.96
USSR	13.43	0.50	-	-	-	-	-	-	-	-	915.38	192.83
Japan	-	-	2.38	0.20	40.38	2.98	16.75	2.53	88.80	20.21	49.27	9.90
Malaysia	-	-	0.20	0.02	-	-	2.00	0.30	-	-	-	-
Singapore	-	-	4.49	0.39	13.29	1.11	62.67	8.45	127.13	25.32	18.40	3.66
Philippines	-	-	-	-	-	-	19.02	2.46	221.49	48.42	276.38	54.17
Thailand	-	-	-	-	-	-	2.99	0.37	-	-	103.43	21.12
Argentina	8.71	0.71	1.09	0.11	8.96	0.94	-	-	-	-	-	-
Latin America	-	-	-	-	-	-	-	-	-	-	34.53	7.42
Middle East	-	-	-	-	-	-	11.17	1.72	191.54	37.31	308.71	65.18
Africa	-	-	-	-	-	-	22.54	3.59	44.55	8.81	137.00	30.79
Others	6.66	0.34	0.63	0.05	35.86	4.64	9.24	1.41	128.40	26.88	168.88	32.79
Total Exports	303.04	19.90	225.03	18.16	981.86	76.63	3256.00	477.99	6917.00	1501.04	8131.00	1677.69

Source: Commodity Statistics, United Nations N.Y.

Table 8-11   Soybean Oil Exports from Brazil by Destination

Destination	1975 Quantity (000 MT)	1975 Value US $M	1980 Quantity (000 MT)	1980 Value US $M	1982 Quantity (000 MT)	1982 Value US $M
Europe(EEC-9)	7.28	4.68	63.44	35.63	12.69	5.64
Spain	2.70	2.42	1.61	1.20	–	–
Eastern Europe	8.15	4.28	42.89	23.21	5.00	2.18
USSR	–	–	32.05	16.94	74.38	33.34
Asia	27.63	15.25	351.41	194.66	377.37	176.00
Latin America	37.95	21.82	16.39	9.61	41.20	18.15
Middle East	120.57	67.88	218.07	125.16	255.06	110.41
Africa	57.02	35.04	18.06	14.85	63.79	34.02
Others	3.17	2.22	0.00	0.00	6.13	-6.56
Total Exports	264.48	153.59	743.92	421.25	835.63	373.18

Source: Commodity Statistics, United Nations N.Y.

took only small quantities.   By 1980 the main outlets were the Middle East and Europe.

The relative importance of each region for each product is shown in Table 8-12.   Examining the proportions exported to each region as a percentage of their total value clarifies the great importance to Brazil of Western Europe as the leading purchaser of both soybeans and meal during the 1970s, but also shows the emergence of the Eastern European nations. Table 8-13 combines the total value of soybean and soybean derivative exports to each region, expressing them again as a percentage of the total.   Looking at these numbers, the relative decline in importance of Western Europe as a market for Brazil, and the growth of Eastern Europe, Asia and the Middle East becomes more evident.

Growth in the world market for fats and oils is closely related to income and population growth; the growth in demand for soybean products very much followed that trend, and is likely to continue to do so.   While capitalizing on the strong growth in demand, in particular for soybean meal, in Western Europe during the rapid build-up of the livestock product markets during the 1970s, Brazil was also able to take advantage of the development of new markets in regions where incomes were beginning to grow.   This was translated into a growing demand for livestock products.

Table 8-12   Brazilian Soybean and Soybean Derivative
                        Exports: Distribution by Region
                        (Percentage of Total Value)

Soybeans

Destination	1965	1970	1975	1980	1982
West Europe	98.32	79.59	84.07	85.37	8.95
East Europe	0.00	20.41	0.02	0.00	0.00
USSR	0.00	0.00	12.66	8.48	51.16
Middle East	0.00	0.00	0.00	0.00	0.00
Asia & Oceana	1.68	0.00	2.86	2.69	2.57
North America	0.00	0.00	0.39	0.00	0.00
Latin America	0.00	0.00	0.00	3.39	37.32
Africa	0.00	0.00	0.00	0.07	0.00
World	100.00	100.00	100.00	100.00	100.00

Soybean Meal

Destination	1965	1970	1975	1980	1985
West Europe	93.67	81.18	63.61	68.87	58.27
East Europe	0.00	7.37	32.19	20.04	17.18
USSR	0.00	0.00	0.00	0.00	11.50
Middle East	0.00	0.00	0.36	2.49	3.88
Asia & Oceana	2.54	6.34	2.98	8.01	6.89
North America	0.00	3.64	0.07	0.00	0.00
Latin America	3.79	1.47	0.04	0.00	0.44
Africa	0.00	0.00	0.75	0.59	1.84
World	100.00	100.00	100.00	100.00	100.00

Soybean Oil

Destination	1965	1970	1975	1980	1985
West Europe			4.51	8.76	1.51
East Europe			2.79	5.52	0.58
USSR			0.00	4.03	8.93
Middle East			44.20	29.78	29.59
Asia & Oceana			10.40	46.08	45.41
North America			1.09	0.00	0.00
Latin America			14.21	2.29	4.86
Africa			22.81	3.53	9.12
World			100.00	100.00	100.00

Source: Commodity Statistics, United Nations, N.Y.

Table 8-13   Distribution of Exports by Region: Soybeans
and Soybean Derivatives (Percentage of Total Value)
(Sum of All Products)

Destination	1965	1970	1975	1980	1982
West Europe	94.93	80.77	67.36	60.76	45.73
East Europe	0.00	10.77	12.02	14.00	13.36
USSR	0.00	0.00	6.59	2.17	13.31
Middle East	0.00	0.00	5.29	7.02	8.08
Asia & Oceana	2.31	4.69	3.78	14.02	13.25
North America	0.00	2.69	0.35	0.00	0.00
Latin America	2.76	1.08	1.67	0.99	3.29
Africa	0.00	0.00	2.93	1.03	2.98
World	100.00	100.00	100.00	100.00	100.00

Source: Commodity Statistics, United Nations, N.Y.

_____

[1] Soybean equivalents includes raw beans plus the amount of beans necessary to produce the volume of soybean products traded on the world market; calculated as 1 ton of beans producing .77 tons of meal, 1 ton of beans producing .17 tons of oil.

9
Summary and Conclusions

SUMMARY

The central objective of this work was to analyze the impact of agricultural diversification through the rapid and substantial expansion of a non-traditional export crop upon the agricultural and economic development of a less-developed country. As a case study, the expansion of soybeans in Brazil was examined. There were six main objectives:

1. To identify the policy background which provided the environment for the soybean expansion.
2. To trace the history of that expansion.
3. To identify the significant resources involved.
4. To examine the contribution of soybeans to Brazil's foreign trade.
5. To assess the distributive effects upon the Brazilian rural population.
6. To explore some of the alternative options which were open to the Brazilian Government within the objectives of promoting economic development.

The first four chapters of this volume gave an account of the background and development of the Brazilian soybean crop. Chapter 1 provided a brief background of the important physical and geographical characteristics of Brazil together with an overview of the general economic development of the country. It showed how these factors have a continuing effect on Brazil's contemporary economic progress and relate directly to the potential for agricultural expansion. The country's historic settlement pattern, the social and political infrastructure which was left behind after colonial rule, and the past experiences of being heavily dependent on brief and dramatic export-led booms, have all had a significant influence on contemporary policy making. Furthermore, the considerable regional differences in population and distribution of wealth and land, together with differing rates of regional development, were shown to have led to some of the acute problems in terms of social equity within Brazil.

Chapter 2 examined some of the theories that have evolved and are recorded in the literature on the contribution of agriculture to economic development. Several theories that have become classics in economic literature have a direct application to Brazil. This study has sought, through the history of the Brazilian soybean expansion, to link reality with economic theory.

Chapter 3 provided an account of Brazilian agricultural policy initiatives, and described the economic environment in which such a rapid expansion of a single crop could take place. This chapter gave an account of the policy background following World War II, Brazil's concentration on forcing the pace of industrialization through the medium of import substitution, and the relative neglect of the agricultural sector, which led to the eventual crisis which overcame agriculture in the early 1960s.

The volume then went on to examine the period following the food crisis, and the policy instruments which were introduced or made more effective to deal with the shortcomings of Brazilian agriculture. In particular, the minimum price policy was strengthened, and very substantial amounts of heavily subsidized rural credit were pumped into the agricultural sector. Rural credit at low or negative rates of interest became the backbone of Brazilian agricultural support. However, the massive flow of credit to a minority of farmers, the heavy bias toward export crops (of which soybeans were by far the greatest recipient—and hence South and Southeast regions) had a very severe impact on the distribution of rural income, both between and within regions. Modern inputs, in the form of fertilizers and tractors, were subject to varying government support schemes at different times. Prior to 1960 there had been a considerable degree of support for imports of both these inputs, particularly through a system of multiple rates of exchange. The early 1960s saw a considerable degree of support for the domestic tractor industry and later the domestic fertilizer

industry. Phosphate, the major nutrient in soybean cultivation, was particularly heavily supported.

The one crop which benefited from the Brazilian ISI
policy was wheat. The encouragement for wheat production was
subsequently to have a profound effect on the early expansion
of the soybean crop, particularly in Rio Grande do Sul, the
state producing the bulk of Brazil's wheat crop. This came
about first, through double cropping, and second by the
utilization of the same production infrastructure.

Although the distribution of land was a fundamental
problem within Brazilian agriculture, structural change was
never a priority in the policy process. From time to time,
efforts were made to deal with the distribution question
through taxation; however, the results appear to have been
negligible. Agricultural research has received more attention in recent years, as has education and extension, but
still requires considerable attention in Brazil.

Chapter 4 looked at the course of the development of the
soybean industry in Brazil from its earliest beginnings to
the major crop it became in the late 1970s and early 1980s.
It described the growth of the crop in Brazilian agriculture,
and its regional distribution and the impact it made on the
agriculture of the two most important soybean growing states,
Rio Grande do Sul and Parana.

The following four chapters gave an account of the
impact, both micro and macro, on the relevant segments of the
Brazilian economy. The first section of Chapter 5 described
how the soybean crop impacted on land use, the distribution
of land, and the pattern of cropping. The area of arable
crops grew by 21.36 percent between 1960 and 1970, and by
44.08 percent during the subsequent decade. Of the absolute
increase of 15.02 million hectares in the 1970-1980 period,
7.46 million, virtually half, was accounted for by the
soybean expansion.

Chapter 5 goes on to describe one of the most evident
consequences of the soybean expansion in the changes in
cropping pattern. This was particularly evident in the
decline in the production of domestic staple crops in the
main soybean-producing areas, including the frontier state of
Mato Grosso. Rio Grande do Sul experienced a 20 percent
decline in domestic staples, and Parana experienced 11.5
percent. Perhaps more significant for the general picture of
Brazil's agriculture was the decline in the production of
domestic staples in terms of production per head of the
population during the height of the soybean expansion. The
two crops most important in the diet of the population of
Brazil's poorer Northeast region, cassava and beans, both

showed absolute declines in production per head over the
country as a whole. The output of rice showed a marginal
increase. Only corn showed any significant improvement.

The agrarian structure in Brazil has many implications
in the sphere of development; this is an area which has long
been held responsible for both the disappointing performance
in sections of Brazilian agriculture and for the maintenance
of profound differences in income, wealth, and equity within
the rural population. The figures showing the distribution
of farm land for the years 1960, 1970, and 1980 show a very
skewed picture, with little meaningful difference between the
two periods. This indicates that the substantial growth in
agriculture in general, and the expansion of soybeans in
particular, did little to improve the agrarian structure
within Brazil.

It was shown that a somewhat different picture emerges
when the data for two main soybean states are examined. Both
states show a small decline in the holdings of under 10
hectares, but significantly there was an increase in the 100
hectare-and-over group. To some extent one may assume that
this is related to the large increase in mechanized soybean
production. This is borne out by the data on the soybean
plantings, as percentage of all crops, on farms growing
soybeans. The data for both Rio Grande do Sul and Parana
showed a growing dependence on the soybean crop in both
states. This was particularly significant in the latter
state, where the level of dependence on soybeans had reached
over 60 percent for all farms under 1000 hectares which
produced soybeans.

Chapter 5 also sought to analyze the technological
implications of the soybean expansion and the relative technical improvement, as measured by increasing yields, for
other crops. All the major crops with the exception of
soybeans, corn, sugar, oranges, and to a small extent
tobacco, showed that yield was a negative contributor to
output growth. Even for soybeans, the contribution was only
10.54 percent with the 89.46 percent remainder coming from
growth in area.

With respect to soybeans, the technological success in
the extensive expansion in area was an achievement in itself.
However, for the remaining crops, the low technical improvement was disappointing and underscored the lack of research
and extension applied to the domestic staple sector. In
terms of utilization of modern inputs, both fertilizers and
tractors experienced considerable growth.

The increasing use of tractors in the soybean areas was
reflected in the out-migration of the rural population. In

Rio Grande do Sul and Parana, between 1970 and 1980, the rural population fell at annual rates of -2.07 and -3.32 respectively. This is of some importance when compared with Brazil's Northeast region. In the Northeast, the proportion of people living in rural areas fell as a proportion of all Brazilian rural dwellers, but the proportion of rural dwellers in the Northeast relative to the total population in that area increased. During this period, Brazil's urban population mushroomed, with the total increase exceeding 28 million or more than 54.5 percent, representing an annual growth rate of 6.96 percent.

Chapter 6 examined the implications of the soybean expansion on secondary production. Of major importance was the emphasis placed on retaining the value-added component of soybean products within Brazil, and the consequent establishment of a substantial crushing capacity. This came about through deterrents on whole soybean exports and generous financial incentives, both to finance the construction of new plant and to provide working capital.

The forward linkages in terms of employment were only marginal, with much of the new modern crushing capacity requiring only a small labor component. Greater benefits were obtained from the contribution to the secondary food industry. Soybean oil became a major source of cooking oil, and domestic availability of soybean meal had a significant influence on the growth of the Brazilian poultry industry.

The contribution of agricultural exports to Brazil's foreign earnings was dealt with in Chapter 7. Although the relative importance of agricultural products as a proportion of all exports was to fall substantially between 1960 and 1980, the part played by soybeans—negligible prior to 1964—grew to nearly 18 percent in 1976, surpassing coffee in importance.

Chapter 7 also examined some of the implications for the distribution of income. It is evident that while there was some reduction in the disparity between sectors, with the gap between rural and urban mean incomes falling (largely due to agriculture retaining its contribution to GDP but with its proportion of the labor force falling) there is strong evidence of increasing disparities within the agricultural sector. The very substantial participation of soybeans to agricultural growth was an important contributor to the growth in farm incomes but, with the crop confined to specific areas and larger farms, it was also an important contributor to the increasing income disparity within the agricultural sector. The distribution of credit was also found to be a major determinant of income disparity, with soybean growers again being the major beneficiaries.

Finally, Chapter 8 dealt with the position of Brazil's soybean exports in the world market. By 1980 Brazil was producing nearly 14 percent of the world's soybeans. In terms of soybean equivalents, Brazil's share of the world market grew from less than 1 percent in 1964 to nearly 17 percent by 1980, during a period when world demand soared. By 1982, Brazil had overtaken the United States in the export of soybean meal, achieving a 40 percent share of the world market. With soybean oil, Brazil achieved a quarter of the world market. The highest absolute growth in demand for soybeans and soybean meal came from Europe, from the EEC for soybeans and from both Western and Eastern Europe for meal.

CONCLUSIONS

What conclusions might one draw from the foregoing analysis? The concept of economic dualism as set out in the literature review was shown to be very significant in Brazil. The growth of the Brazilian economy over the period of this study does not appear inconsistent with the Lewis-Ranis and Fei growth models. The acute problem in Brazil was, and remain, the bridging of the gap between the traditional and non-traditional economies. Much of the problem is still closely associated with human capital development and, although great strides have been made, the study showed that this was not a policy priority in Brazil. The rapid growth of a non-traditional crop,. utilizing available resources which were surplus to the country's domestic requirements, was shown to be closely in accordance with Myint's "vent for surplus" model. The enormous success of the soybean expansion should be weighed against the drawbacks. It is clear that the linkages formed within the soybean economy are with the modern sector rather than the traditional, and although, as suggested above, the crop contributed substantially to agricultural growth and the increase of average farm incomes, it in fact deepened the divisions within agriculture and between regional rural populations.

The soybean technology which was available to Brazil in the early 1960s was developed for a very different set of constraints. Whereas a technology may be readily transfer-able in terms of land and climate, the situation between developed and less-developed countries--in this case the United States and Brazil--may be totally different. Such as the availability, and hence the relative costs, of labor and capital.

Doubts about the degree of appropriateness appear well borne out by the results. Modern soybean technology is largely based on the development of agriculture in advanced countries where the agricultural sector was called on to supply a rapidly growing industrial demand for labor; the situation in Brazil is very different with the urban population growing at a rate far faster than industry can absorb. When the United States had reached a similar stage of development to that Brazil reached by the 1970s, the industrial world was then facing a future of huge industrial concerns with a seemingly insatiable demand for labor; industries such as textiles, ship building, steel production, and the automobile industry to name but a few. Industrialization in the 1980s differs both in product mix and level of technology, and hence in labor requirements. In the words of one author, there has been an "uncoupling" of the traditional industrial growth-employment relationship (Drucker, 1985). Modern industrial growth requires a far lower labor content, and this has serious implications for Brazil as it has for developing countries in general.

Furthermore, the future of world markets for primary products is very uncertain, with producers once more facing declining terms of trade for their output. The level of dependence of Brazilian agriculture on a single export crop whose ultimate destination is largely to producers of dairy and other livestock products (much of which are in considerable surplus in the developed economies) could present problems in the not-too-distant future, and may impact heavily upon soybean farms.

The concentration on agricultural growth through the expansion of a non-traditional crop has been shown to have had serious implications for the traditional sector of agriculture. Not only has investment in human capital been restricted, but much of the research investment has been diverted to soybeans at the expense of the domestic crops on which the poorer groups in Brazilian society so depend. Brazil turned its back on strengthening the position of domestic crops through research which might have led to lower food prices and higher productivity. For a country which saw enormous industrial growth in the 1970s and which has become a significant world industrial power, a substantial proportion of the population in the 1980s still suffer some degree of malnourishment, including almost half the children (Grey, 1982). The problem exists in the poor rural communities but it is even more serious among the growing number of urban poor.

Any potential benefit from redistribution of land remains an open question. As has been shown, much of Brazil's agricultural growth has been independent of policies to absorb labor within agriculture; agricultural growth has pushed and continues to push many toward the urban conurbations without regard to employment prospects. There is conflicting evidence to support the view that land reform necessarily reduces either output or productivity, in fact the converse has been shown to be the case (Dovring, 1970).

Part of the question surrounds the determinants of "social" as opposed to "private" benefit. Much of the benefit derived from the expansion of soybeans in Brazil has gone to existing landowners, and urban industrialists in the South and Southeast of the country. Much of the social costs have been borne by other sectors of the population. In Brazil, as in much of Latin America, the political infrastructure is such that landowners have a strong vested interest in maintaining the status quo.

The expansion of soybean production in Brazil has been an amazing achievement, but it was facilitated by three overriding and interdependent factors: a favorable world market and the consequent price incentives, a readily available technology, and a favorable policy environment.

There appears to have been no clear social objectives either in the case of the Brazilian government or the providers of economic aid. Indeed, it is conceivable that concentration on the expansion of a single export crop, although contributing substantially to economic growth (and even to an extent economic development) actually widened the gulf between the traditional and modern sectors, which could lead in turn to a degree of political destabilization.

In the case of the United States, its own objectives in Brazil's soybean expansion program are even more nebulous. The United States's generosity in providing the technology (developed with great efforts and at substantial public cost) which eventually was to lead to the sacrifice of part of its share of the world market for soybeans and soybean products, is indisputable. The degree to which the implications of such aid were considered remains unclear. It would seem that those with the responsibility of formulating policies, whether governments dealing with domestic agriculture or institutions providing international aid, should address these questions somewhere within the process.

This study set out to examine some of the issues involved in the promotion of a non-traditional crop as a means of furthering economic development. The case of the Brazilian soybean expansion provides a valuable insight into the high level of success in terms of agricultural expansion and economic growth, but the beneficial impact upon development is less clear. The extent to which the experience of Brazil can be generalized to other development situations is even less evident. However, it does provide a valuable guide to the effects, should the conditions be favorable, of superimposing a modern agricultural technology on an agriculture which still contains a very large traditional element.

Appendix

LIST OF APPENDIX TABLES

Table A5-1   Brazil: Production of Cassava, 1960-82

Year	Area (000 Ha)	Yield (Kg/Ha)	Production (000 MT)	Brazil Pop. (Mill)	Production Kgs. per Head
1960	1,342	13,100	17,613	70	252.6
1961	1,414	13,000	18,407	72	255.9
1962	1,476	13,400	19,843	75	265.6
1963	1,618	13,800	22,249	77	290.7
1964	1,716	14,200	24,356	79	309.4
1965	1,750	14,300	24,993	81	308.5
1966	1,780	13,900	24,710	83	298.0
1967	1,914	14,300	27,268	85	319.9
1968	1,998	14,600	29,203	88	333.3
1969	2,029	14,800	30,074	90	333.9
1970	2,025	14,553	29,464	93	318.5
1971	2,050	14,762	30,258	95	317.9
1972	2,100	14,762	31,000	98	316.8
1973	2,119	12,580	26,653	101	265.0
1974	2,008	12,309	24,715	103	239.1
1975	2,098	12,300	25,812	106	243.0
1976	2,112	12,698	26,816	108	249.4
1977	2,176	11,919	25,929	110	235.3
1978	2,202	11,514	25,358	113	224.5
1979	2,105	11,884	25,935	116	224.1
1980	2,016	11,614	23,466	121	193.5
1981	2,088	11,881	24,803	124	200.0
1982	2,110	11,605	24,492	127	193.1

Source: Calculated from Anuario Estatistico, Rio de Janeiro:
        IBGE, various years.

Table A5-2 Brazil: Changes in Production of Cassava, 1960-82
(1960 = 100)

Year	Area (000 Ha)	Yield (Kg/Ha)	Production (000 MT)	Brazil Pop. (Mill)	Production Kgs. per Head
1960	100	100	100	100	100
1961	105	99	105	103	101
1962	110	102	113	107	105
1963	121	105	126	110	115
1964	128	108	138	113	122
1965	130	109	142	116	122
1966	133	106	140	119	118
1967	143	109	155	122	127
1968	149	111	166	126	132
1969	151	113	171	129	132
1970	151	111	167	133	126
1971	153	113	172	137	126
1972	156	113	176	140	125
1973	158	96	151	144	105
1974	150	94	140	148	95
1975	156	94	147	152	96
1976	157	97	152	154	99
1977	162	91	147	158	93
1978	164	88	144	162	89
1979	157	91	147	166	89
1980	150	89	133	174	77
1981	156	91	141	178	79
1982	157	89	139	182	76

Source: Calculated from Anuario Estatistico, Rio de Janeiro:
IBGE, various years. Source: As Table A5-1

Table A5-3   Brazil: Production of Beans, 1960-82

Year	Area (000 Ha)	Yield (Kg/Ha)	Production (000 MT)	Brazil Pop. (Mill)	Production Kgs. per Head
1960	2,581	680	1,744	69.72	25
1961	2,716	630	1,710	71.94	24
1962	2,982	650	1,942	74.71	26
1963	3,130	620	1,942	76.53	25
1964	3,131	620	1,951	78.73	25
1965	3,273	700	2,290	81.01	28
1966	3,325	650	2,148	82.93	26
1967	3,651	700	2,548	85.24	30
1968	3,663	660	2,420	87.62	28
1969	3,633	610	2,200	90.07	24
1970	3,485	635	2,241	92.52	24
1971	3,743	668	2,500	95.17	26
1972	3,700	643	2,380	97.85	24
1973	3,788	584	2,211	100.56	22
1974	4,293	521	2,238	103.35	22
1975	4,143	548	2,271	106.23	21
1976	3,985	483	1,923	107.54	18
1977	4,551	503	2,290	110.21	21
1978	4,586	477	2,188	112.94	19
1979	4,212	519	2,187	115.74	19
1980	4,643	424	1,268	121.29	10
1981	5,031	465	2,339	124.02	19
1982	5,987	493	2,951	126.81	23

Source: Calculated from Anuario Estatistico, Rio de Janeiro:
        IBGE, various years.

Table A5-4 Brazil: Changes in Production of Beans, 1960-82
(1960 = 100)

Year	Area (000 Ha)	Yield (Kg/Ha)	Production (000 MT)	Brazil Pop. (Mill)	Production (Kgs/Head)
1960	100	100	100	100	100
1961	105	93	98	103	95
1962	116	96	111	107	104
1963	121	91	111	110	101
1964	121	91	112	113	99
1965	127	103	131	116	113
1966	129	96	123	119	104
1967	141	103	146	122	119
1968	142	97	139	126	110
1969	141	90	126	129	98
1970	135	93	128	133	97
1971	145	98	143	137	105
1972	143	95	136	140	97
1973	147	86	127	144	88
1974	166	77	128	148	87
1975	161	81	130	152	85
1976	154	71	110	154	71
1977	176	74	131	158	83
1978	178	70	125	162	77
1979	163	76	125	166	76
1980	180	62	73	174	42
1981	195	68	134	178	75
1982	232	73	169	182	93

Source: Calculated from Anuario Estatistico, Rio de Janeiro: IBGE, various years.

Table A5-5   Brazil: Production of Rice, 1960-82

Year	Area (000 Ha)	Yield (Kg/Ha)	Production (000 MT)	Brazil Pop. (Mill).	Production Kgs per Head
1960	2,966	1,617	4,795	70	68.8
1961	3,174	1,699	5,392	72	75.0
1962	3,350	1,659	5,557	75	74.4
1963	3,722	1,542	5,740	77	75.0
1964	4,182	1,517	6,345	79	80.6
1965	4,619	1,641	7,580	81	93.6
1966	4,005	1,449	5,802	83	70.0
1967	4,291	1,583	6,792	85	79.7
1968	4,459	1,492	6,653	88	75.9
1969	4,621	1,384	6,394	90	71.0
1970	4,979	1,517	7,553	93	81.6
1971	4,764	1,384	6,593	95	69.3
1972	4,821	1,623	7,824	98	80.0
1973	4,795	1,493	7,160	101	71.2
1974	4,665	1,390	6,483	103	62.7
1975	5,306	1,421	7,538	106	71.0
1976	6,656	1,436	9,560	108	88.9
1977	5,992	1,218	7,296	110	66.2
1978	5,624	1,350	7,595	113	67.2
1979	5,452	1,788	9,748	116	84.2
1980	6,243	1,566	9,776	121	80.6
1981	6,102	1,349	8,228	124	66.3
1982	6,024	1,616	9,735	127	76.8

Source: Calculated from Anuario Estatistico, Rio de Janeiro: IBGE, various years.

Table A5-6   Brazil: Changes in Production of Rice, 1960-82
(1960 = 100)

Year	Area (000 Ha)	Yield (Kg/Ha)	Production (000 MT)	Brazil Pop. (Mill).	Production Kgs per Head
1960	100	100	100	100	100
1961	107	105	112	103	109
1962	113	103	116	107	108
1963	125	95	120	110	109
1964	141	94	132	113	117
1965	156	102	158	116	136
1966	135	90	121	119	102
1967	145	98	142	122	116
1968	150	92	139	126	110
1969	156	86	133	129	103
1970	168	94	158	133	119
1971	161	86	138	137	101
1972	163	100	163	140	116
1973	162	92	149	144	104
1974	157	86	135	148	91
1975	179	88	157	152	103
1976	224	89	199	154	129
1977	190	75	152	158	96
1978	188	84	158	162	98
1979	184	111	203	166	122
1980	210	97	204	174	117
1981	206	83	172	178	96
1982	203	100	203	182	112

Source: Calculated from Anuario Estatistico, Rio de Janeiro:
IBGE, various years.

Table A5-7   Brazil: Production of Corn, 1960-82

Year	Area (000 Ha)	Yield (Kg/Ha)	Production (000 MT)	Brazil Pop. (Mil)	Production Kgs per Head
1960	6,681	1,298	8,672	69.72	124.4
1961	6,886	1,312	9,036	71.94	125.6
1962	7,348	1,305	9,587	74.71	128.3
1963	7,958	1,309	10,418	76.53	136.1
1964	8,106	1,161	9,408	78.73	119.5
1965	8,771	1,381	12,112	81.01	149.5
1966	8,703	1,307	11,371	82.93	137.1
1967	9,274	1,383	12,824	85.24	150.4
1968	9,584	1,337	12,814	87.62	146.2
1969	9,654	1,315	12,693	90.07	140.9
1970	9,858	1,442	14,216	92.52	153.7
1971	10,709	1,336	14,307	95.17	150.3
1972	10,539	1,413	14,891	97.85	152.2
1973	9,914	1,418	14,059	100.56	139.8
1974	10,294	1,294	16,285	103.35	157.6
1975	10,473	1,562	16,354	106.23	153.9
1976	11,122	1,612	17,929	107.54	166.7
1977	11,797	1,632	19,256	110.21	174.7
1978	11,084	1,221	13,533	112.94	119.8
1979	11,214	1,442	16,039	115.74	138.6
1980	11,451	1,779	20,372	121.29	168.0
1981	11,493	1,836	21,098	124.02	170.1
1982	12,650	1,733	21,919	126.81	172.8

Source: Calculated from Anuario Estatistico, Rio de Janeiro: IBGE, various years.

Table A5-8   Brazil: Changes in Production of Corn, 1960-82
(1960 = 100)

Year	Area (000 Ha)	Yield (Kg/Ha)	Production (000 MT)	Brazil Pop. (Mil)	Production Kgs per Head
1960	100	100	100	100	100
1961	103	101	104	103	101
1962	110	101	111	107	103
1963	119	101	120	110	109
1964	121	89	108	113	96
1965	131	106	140	116	120
1966	130	101	131	119	110
1967	139	107	148	122	121
1968	143	103	148	126	118
1969	144	101	146	129	113
1970	148	111	164	133	124
1971	160	103	165	137	121
1972	158	109	172	140	122
1973	148	109	162	144	112
1974	154	100	188	148	127
1975	157	120	189	152	124
1976	166	124	207	154	134
1977	177	126	222	158	140
1978	166	94	156	162	96
1979	168	111	185	166	111
1980	171	137	235	174	135
1981	172	141	243	178	137
1982	189	134	253	182	139

Source: Derived from Annuario Estatistico—Various Issues
        —IBGE.

References

Adams, Dale, et al. Farm Growth in Brazil. Columbus, Ohio:
The Ohio State Unversity, 1979.

Alves, Elseu Roberto de Andrade, and Pastore, Affonse Celso.
"Import Substitution and Implicit Taxation of Agriculture in Brazil." Amer. J. Agr. Econ. 60 (1978): 865-871.

Baer, Werner. The Brazilian Economy: Growth and Development.
New York: Praeger, 1983.

Bowman, John E. "Characterization of Soybean Expansion and
Consequent Agricultural Changes in the State of Parana,
Brazil 1970-1980." Londrina: Centro Nacional de Pesquisa
de Soja, Londrina, 1983.

Broadbent, E., and Parry Dixon, F. "Exploratory Study of
Brazilian Soybean Marketing." AER-144. Urbana: University of Illinois Agricultural Experimental Station,
1976.

Chacel, Julian. "Agrarian Structure and Agricultural Production." In The Economy of Brazil, ed. H. Ellis.
Berkeley: University of California Press, 1969.

da Mata, Milton. "Credito Rural: Characterizacao do Sistema e
Estimatives dos Subsidos Implicitos." Rev. Bras. Econ.
36 (July-September, 1982): 215-245.

de Janvry, Alain. "The Political Economy of Rural Development
in Latin America: An Interpretation." Amer. J. of Agr.
Economics, 57 (1975): 490-499.

Denslow, David, and Tyler, William. "Perspectives on Poverty
and Income Inequality in Brazil." World Development 12
(1984): 1019-1028.

Dovring, F. "Land Reform And Productivity in Mexico." Land
Economics 46 (August 1970): 264-274.

_____. "Underemployment, Slow motion and X-efficiency." Economic Development and Cultural Change. 27 (April 1979): 485-490.

_____. "Capital and Productivity in Agriculture." Urbana: University of Illinois, 1982 (Unpublished mimeograph).

Drefus, S. A. Louis et Cie., "Brazilian Soybean Complex." Paris: S.A. Louis Drefus & Cie, 1984, (Unpublished mimeograph).

Drucker, Peter F. "The Changed World Economy." Foreign Affairs. 64 (Spring 1986): 768-779.

Duran, Tulio Arvelo. "Brazilian Government Policies in Agriculture: The Case of Grains and Soybeans." Ph.D. thesis, University of Chicago, 1979.

D'Utra, Gustavo. "Soja." Jornal do Agroculture (Setembro 1882).

F.A.O. Production Year Book. Rome: Food and Agricultural Organization of the United Nations, various years.

_____. Trade Year Book. Rome: Food and Agricultural Organization of the United Nations, various years.

Fields, Gary S. "Who Benefits from Economic Development?--A Reexamination of Brazilian Growth in the 1960's." The American Economic Review. 67 (September 1977): 570-581.

Fox, Roger. "Brazil's Minimum Price Policy and The Agricultural Sector of Northeast Brazil." International Food Policy Research Institute: Research Report 9, June 1979.

Fundacao IBGE. Anuario Estatistico do Brazil. Rio de Janiero: IBGE, various issues.

_____. Censo Agropecuario, 1970. Rio de Janeiro: IBGE, 1970.

_____. Censo Agropecuario, 1975. Rio de Janeiro: IBGE, 1979.

_____. Censo Agropecuario, 1980. Rio de Janeiro: IBGE, 1984.

_____. Censo demographico de 1970. Rio de Janeiro: IBGE, 1970.

_____. Censo demographico de 1980. Rio de Janeiro: IBGE, 1980.

_____. Crescimento e Distribuicao da Populacao Brasileira. 1940-1980. Rio de Janeiro: IBGE, 1980.

Furtado, Celso. The Economic Growth of Brazil. Berkeley: University of California Press, 1971.

Ghatak, S. and Ingersent, K. Agriculture and Economic Development. Baltimore: John Hopkins University Press, 1984.

Grey, Cheryl Williamson. "Food Consumption Parameters for Brazil and their Application to Food Policy." International Food Policy Research Institute, Research Report 32, September, 1982.

Gulliver, K. "The Brazilian Soybean Economy: An Econometric Model with Emphasis on Government Policy." Unpublished Ph.D. thesis, University of Minnesota, 1981.

Hartwig, Edgar E. "Observations relative to Soybean Research in Brazil." Rio de Janeiro: USAID Office of Agriculture and Rural Development, 1966. Mimeograph.

Henshall, Janet D. and Momsen, R. P. A Geography of Brazilian Development. London: G. Bell & Sons, 1974.

Homem de Melo, Fernando. "Economic Policy and the Agricultural Sector in Brazil." Luso-Brazilian Review. 14 (1978): 114-126.

_____. "Export Agriculture and the Problem of Food Production." Brazilian Economic Studies. 7 (1983) 1-19.

_____. "Distributive Implications of the Growth of Soybean Production in Brazil." Paper presented to the World Soybean Conference, Ames Iowa, 1984.

Houck, James P., Ryan, Mary E., and Subotnik, Abraham. Soybeans and Their Products: Markets, Models and Policy. Minneapolis: University of Minnesota Press, 1972.

Hyami, Y., and Ruttan, V. W. Agricultural Development: An International Perspective, Baltimore: The John Hopkins University Press, Baltimore, 1971, 20-21.

Hymowitz et al, "The Brazilian Soybean Program." Soybean Digest 28 (May 1968): 62-65.

International Monetory Fund. International Financial Statistics. Washington, D.C: IMF, various issues.

Knight, Peter T. Brazilian Agricultural Technology and Trade. New York: Preager Publishers Inc., 1971.

Lewis, W. A. "Economic Development with Unlimited Supplies of Labor." The Manchester School of Economics and Social Studies. 22 (May 1954): 139-193.

_____."The Dual Economy Revisited." The Manchester School of Economics and Social Studies. 47 (Sept. 1979): 211-229.

Mellor, John. "Towards a Theory of Agricultural Development." Agricultural Development and Economic Growth, ed. Herman Southworth and Bruce Johnson. Ithica: Cornell University Press, Ithaca, 1967.

Myint, H. "The Classical Theory of International Trade and The Underdeveloped Countries." Economic Journal. 68 (June 1958): 317-337.

Nicholls, William H. "The Brazilian Agricultural Economy: Recent Performance and Policy." In Brazil in the Sixties, ed. Riordan Roett, Nasville: Vanderbuilt University Press, Nashville, 1972.

_____. "The Transformation of Agriculture in a Semi-Industrialized Country: The Case of Brazil." In The Role of Agriculture in Economic Development, ed. Erik Thorbecke, New York: National Bureau of Economic Research, 1969.

_____. "Agriculture and the Economic Development of Brazil." In Modern Brazil, ed. John Saunders, Gainsville: University of Florida Press, 1971.

Paiva, Ruy Miller., et al. Brazil's Agricultural Sector, Economic Behavior, Problems and Possibilities. Sao Paulo: Proceedings of the xv International Conference of Agricultural Economists, 1973.

Prado, Junior Caio, The Colonial Background of Modern Brazil. Berkeley: University of California Press, 1967.

Prebisch, Raul. "The Economic Development of Latin America and its Principal Problems." Economic Bulletin for Latin America. 7 (February 1962): 1-22.

_____. Change and Development--Latin America's GreatTask. New York: Preager Publishers, 1970.

_____. "The Latin American Periphery in the Global System of Capitalism." CEPAL Review. 3 (April 1981): 145-150.

Quintana, Flavio. " Rural Productivity on Small Farms in The State of Rio Grande do Sul--Brazil." Unpublished Ph.D. thesis, University of Illinois, Urbana, 1982.

Ranis, G., and Fei J. C. "A Theory of Economic Development." In Agriculture in Economic Development, ed G.K. Eicher and L. W. Witt. New York: McGraw-Hill Book Co., 1964.

Sanders, John H., and Ruttan, Vernon W., "Biased Choice of Technology in Brazilian Agriculture." In Induced Innovation, ed. Hans P. Binswanger, et al. Baltimore: The John Hopkins University Press, 1978.

Sayad, Joao. "The Impact of Rural Credit on Production and Income Distribution in Brazil." In Rural Financial Markets in Developing Countries - Their Uses and Abuses, ed. Von Pischke et al. Baltimore: The John Hopkins University Press, 1979.

Schuh, G. Edward. The Agricultural Development of Brazil. New York: Praeger Publishers, 1970.

Schultz, John M., and Mason, W. P., Soybeans, Brazil as a Competitive Force. Harvard, 1976.

Schultz, Theodore W. Transforming Traditional Agriculture New Haven: Yale University Press, 1964.

Smith, Gordon W. "Brazilian Agicultural Policy, 1950-1967."
    In The Economy of Brazil, ed. H. Ellis. Berkeley:
    University of California Press, 1969.

Soskin, A. B. "An Evaluation of Brazilian Agricultural Policy
    and Its Impact upon the Agricultural Developement of Rio
    Grande do Sul." Unpublished M.S.thesis. University of
    Illinois, Urbana, 1981.

Tendler, Judith. "Agricultural Credit in Brazil."
    Washington, D.C: USAID, 1969. (Mimeograph).

Thompson, Robert L., "The Brazilian Soybean Situation and Its
    Impact on the World Oils Market. "Journal of the Oil
    Chemists Society. 56 (May 1979): 138-148.

Todaro, Michael P. "A Model of Rural Urban Migration and
    Urban Unemployment in Less Developed Countries."
    American Econ. Review 59 (March 1959): 138-148.

United Nations. Commodity Statistics, New York: United
    Nations, various issues.

United Nations. Economic Survey For Latin America, New York:
    United Nations, various issues.

Williams, Gary W., and Thompson R. L., "The Brazilian Soybean
    Industry: Economic Structure and Policy Interventions."
    Washington D.C: USDA, Foreign Agricultural Economic
    Report Number 200, Economic Research Service, 1984a.

_____. "Brazilian Soybean Policy: the Effects of inter-
    vention." Amer. J. Agr. Econ. 66 (Nov. 1984): 488-498.

World Bank. World Bank Development Report 1985. New York:
    Oxford University Press, 1985.

_____. Brazil: A Review of Agricultural Policies.
    Washington, D.C: The World Bank, 1979a.

_____. Brazil: Human Resources Special Report, Washington,
    D.C: The World Bank, 1979.

Zockun, Maria Helena Garcia Pallares, A Expansao Da Soja No
    Brasil: Alguns Aspectos Da Producao, Sao Paulo: Ensaios
    Economicos, 1980.

Index

About the Author

Anthony Soskin was born in Bedfordshire, England. He received a Bachelor of Science degree in agricultural economics from the University of Durham in 1962. After farming for seventeen years in England he moved to the United States. He received a Master of Science degree in 1981, an MBA in 1983, and a Doctorate in 1986, all from the University of Illinois.

Currently he lives in Champaign, Illinois, with his wife and four children.